THE ACTS OF
THE APOSTLES

THE ACTS OF THE APOSTLES

A Companion

**Richard Wallace
and Wynne Williams**

**Published by Bristol Classical Press
General Editor: John H. Betts**

First published in 1993 by
Bristol Classical Press
an imprint of
Gerald Duckworth & Co. Ltd
The Old Piano Factory
48 Hoxton Square, London N1 6PB

A catalogue record for this book is available
from the British Library

ISBN 1-85399-141-4

Available in USA and Canada from:
Focus Information Group
PO Box 369
Newburyport
MA 01950

Printed in Great Britain by
Booksprint, Bristol

For Chloe and Julia

and

For Eiry and Carys

Contents

Preface

Like most of the books of the New Testament, the *Acts of the Apostles* has attracted a formidable amount of scholarly work. Most of it, however, is on the theological issues it raises, or on questions of Church History.

This *Companion* is an attempt to fill a gap which we have discovered during many years of using *Acts* as a set text for a special subject for undergraduates in Classics at Keele. Though many previous works have attempted to illuminate *Acts* by setting it in the context of contemporary history and society, there is no other introductory work which concentrates on *Acts* as a historical source (in the widest sense) in its own right. Our aim is to treat *Acts* seriously as a work of history (and indeed as a uniquely valuable source for the way the Roman Empire in the east worked in the eyes of at least some of its subjects). We have, in so far as it is possible, made every effort to avoid questions of theology.

The translation on which we are commenting is that of the *New English Bible* (NEB), on the grounds that this is the translation which most readers will have easily available. In many cases, however, in the interests of readability, the translators have obscured or skipped over real difficulties in the Greek. Where this has happened we have added the translation of the *Revised Standard Version* (RSV), which is much closer to the original. This translation (or its ecumenical counterpart, the *Common Bible*), is the one which all serious students of *Acts* will want to use.

We wish to thank: our colleagues at Keele, for their encouragement and help; our families for their forbearance; generations of Keele students, for raising the questions which this book tries to answer; and, especially, Bron, our secretary at Keele, who has supported us untiringly, who has kept us sane in bad times, and without whose unobtrusive efficiency, unfailing generosity, and tolerant good-humour, this (and many other things) would never have been done.

We particularly wish to record our debt to Professor A.L.F. Rivet, who for many years set his younger colleagues at Keele an example of scholarly rigour, while demonstrating that rigour was not incompatible with imagination and enthusiasm.

Wynne Williams and Richard Wallace
(Department of Classics, University of Keele)

Introduction

From the point of view of the historian, *The Acts of the Apostles* is perhaps the most interesting and revealing book in the New Testament. When the Christian Church begins to appear in the historical record in the second century, it is already a large, widespread, group, with an efficient organisation, a well-established structure, a hierarchy of officers, its own sacred literature, and a distinctive form of religious cult. It is, in other words, clearly a new religion, distinct not only from paganism, but also from Judaism in which it had its roots. Christianity, within a couple of generations, had ceased to be a Jewish sect, and had instead become a group which was largely Greek-speaking, which appealed almost exclusively to the Gentile world, and which was positively hostile to Judaism. Our evidence for the process whereby this community emerged from the followers of a Jewish teacher, whose activity was restricted to Palestine, and whose teaching was directed almost entirely at Palestinian Jews, comes largely from *Acts*, together with the letters of Paul.

Acts, then, is our major piece of evidence for the extension of Christianity from the Jewish to the Greek world, and for the creation of what was to emerge as a new religion. In addition we are given an invaluable picture of the cities of the eastern half of the Roman empire, which throws a great deal of light on the way in which the empire really worked. *Acts* is unusual in that it is written from the point of view of those who were outside the dominant culture, and who did not identify themselves with the ruling *élite*, and so gives a perspective on government and civic life in the Roman empire which cannot be matched from any other source.

Acts is a work which presents many problems. Its authorship, date, provenance, and purpose are all matters of acute controversy.

I Title and contents

The problems surrounding *Acts* begin with the title. The work is called *The Acts of the Apostles* in the earliest texts which refer to it (e.g. Clement *Strom.* 5.12); it is called *The Acts of All the Apostles* in the Muratorian

Canon (a fragmentary work probably of the late 2nd century, which lists the books of the New Testament canon, and is named after L.A. Muratori, who published it in 1740). The name, however, is entirely inappropriate. The apostles in general ('the twelve') appear only in the earliest chapters; only Peter (sometimes accompanied by John) acts as an individual; after his conversion in ch. 9 Paul rather than the apostles becomes the centre of the narrative. From ch. 13 onwards the other leaders of the community appear only when their activities directly affect Paul. *Acts*, then, concentrates largely on the activities of Paul. However, although Paul in his epistles regularly introduces himself as an apostle, and is emphatic in his claim to the title (e.g. 1 Cor. 9.1-12; 1 Cor. 15.9-10; 2 Cor. 12.11-12), *Acts* regularly represents the apostles as a closed body of twelve (and indeed the first episode recorded is the making up of the number by the election of another member after the defection of Judas Iscariot). In only one episode are Paul and Barnabas referred to (without comment) as apostles (see notes to 14.4 and 14). The traditional title, then, is singularly inappropriate, and it is improbable that it is the original one.

The real subject of *Acts* is Paul, and in particular his rôle as 'apostle to the Gentiles'. Even within these limitations, the author is selective in his use of material. Of the long list of tribulations which Paul claims in his letters to have faced (2 Cor. 11.22-33; they include five floggings, three beatings, a stoning, and three shipwrecks) *Acts* includes only a representative sample (presumably for reasons of space, so that the work could be written in a single volume, that is to say one scroll of papyrus). The author's interests are not primarily biographical. It is the vindication of Paul's mission to the Gentiles which is the central theme of the work, rather than the portrait of Paul himself. We are given sufficient narrative to place what the author represents as the key incidents in that work in an appropriate context, and little else. The activities of the other apostles, and of other important figures such as Barnabas and Apollos, are mentioned only incidentally, although they clearly played a great part in the dissemination of Christianity at this period. We are given no information about the origins of Christian communities, such as those in Egypt and Rome, which were later large and important. *Acts* is not a History of the Church. It is an account of the significant events in the life and work of one man – Paul.

Acts falls into three distinct sections:

1. The prelude to Paul's work (chs 1-12): the beginnings of the church and its early history; the spread of the message to Samaritans (8.5-25) and to Gentiles (Philip and the Ethiopian: 8.26-39; Peter and Cornelius: 10.1-11.18); the beginning of persecution; Paul's conversion and early work.

2. Paul's mission to the Gentiles (chs 13-20): the missionary journeys; the controversy over the admission of Gentiles.

3. The culmination of Paul's work (chs 21-8): Paul's last trip to Jerusalem; his arrest and trials; his journey to Rome.

Within this overall plan, there are a number of themes which run through the work, and which seem to represent the perspective on the early church's history which the author wants to urge upon his readers.

1. The Spirit. The work of the church in spreading its message is guided by the Spirit (e.g. 13.2, 16.6-7). Conversion and belief are marked by the gift of the Spirit (e.g. 19.1-7), and God's acceptance of Gentile converts is proved by the fact that he has given the gift of the Spirit to them, no less than to Jewish converts (e.g. 10.44-8, 15.8).

2. Rome. Roman power is always presented in a favourable light. In no case do the Romans take action against Paul or the other Christians. Trouble arises only from the malicious accusations of the Jews. When brought before Roman officials, Paul is consistently vindicated (by Gallio at 18.14-16; by Festus at 25.25). The governor of Cyprus accepts the Christian message (13.12). At Philippi (16.37-9) and at Ephesus (19.37-40) the power of Rome is invoked to protect Paul and his companions. There is no hint of a persecution initiated by the Romans themselves.

3. The unity of the Church. Although *Acts* deals with controversies within the church, such as the question of the admission of Gentile converts, the stress is always on unity and harmony. There is no hint of the conflicts and vigorous polemic revealed by Paul's letters. The sort of division within the church which is the subject of Paul's letters to the Corinthians or the Galatians has no place in *Acts*.

It is unfortunate that these recurrent themes give no unambiguous clues to the date, context, or purposes of *Acts*. The author's preoccupation with the status of Gentile converts, and his concern over divisions within the community caused by this dispute, could suggest that *Acts* was written when these questions were still alive, and so indicate an early date; the favourable view taken of Rome might be evidence that, at the date of composition, serious persecution had not yet begun. On the other hand, it is no less plausible to argue that what we are given is an idealised picture of life in the church in its earliest days, which the author intended his readers to contrast with the church of his own day; his insistence on good relations between the earliest church and the Roman authorities might constitute an apologetic argument, a claim that at the beginning Christians were consistently found to be without fault in their relations with the state, and hence that later persecutions were based on misunderstandings created by malicious slanders.

The fact that *Acts* is written in Greek, and good Greek, is an indication that the intended audience was itself Greek-speaking, and so part of the Greek rather than the Palestinian/Aramaic world. On the other hand, the author clearly expects his readers to be familiar with the content and style of the Septuagint, the Greek translation of the Old Testament which was widely used in Greek-speaking Jewish communities, and which was universally adopted as the authoritative version by the early church. He also feels able to allude to, rather than explain, central Christian practices and ideas (e.g. 'the breaking of bread' at 2.42). The probability, then, is that the author of *Acts* envisaged as his audience a Greek-speaking Christian community, perhaps one of the Gentile-Christian churches among which Paul had been working. The fact that *Acts*, like the Gospel of Luke, is addressed to an otherwise unknown Theophilus is of little help. The dedication of a work to an individual, although by no means invariable in the ancient world, was quite common. It is usually no more than a way of paying a compliment to a patron (or someone the author hopes will become a patron). It certainly does not signify that the work was written exclusively, or even primarily, for him.

II Date and author

Like the other books in the New Testament (with the exception of those written in epistolary form) and like the historical books of the Old Testament, *Acts* does not tell us who wrote it, or when he wrote it. The preface (1.1-2) is clearly intended to make us believe that the author is the same person as the author of the Gospel of Luke. In view of the striking similarities in the language, style, and approach of the two works there is no reason to doubt this claim.

The fullest statement of the traditional account of the authorship of *Acts* was given at the beginning of the 4th century by Eusebius (*Ecclesiastical History* 3, 4, 6):

> Luke, by origin an Antiochene, and by profession a doctor, was a frequent companion of Paul, and a close associate of the other apostles. He left behind for us examples of the art of healing souls which he obtained from them in two books, inspired by God: the Gospel...and *The Acts of the Apostles*, which he composed, not from reports, but from the evidence of his own eyes.

The identification of the author of *Acts* with Luke, 'the beloved physician' of Col. 4.14 (who is also mentioned in 2 Tim. 4.11 and Phlm. 24), appears first in the second half of the 2nd century, in the Muratorian Canon, the so-called Anti-Marcionite Prologue to Luke, and Irenaeus (esp. *Adv. Haer.* 3, 14, 1). The additional information that Luke was from Antioch is found for the first time in this passage of Eusebius. It is not at all clear whether these reports are based on real information derived from earlier traditions, or whether they are simply inferences drawn from the text of *Acts* itself. Eusebius seems to have found nothing about *Luke* or *Acts* in Papias, his source for information on the composition of *Mark, Matthew,* and *John.* The belief that *Acts* was written by a companion of Paul may be based on nothing more than the occurrence from time to time of the first person in some narratives in *Acts* (the 'we'-passages; see pp. 12-15 below for a fuller discussion). If so, the identification of this supposed eye-witness with Luke may have been arrived at simply by comparing the companions mentioned by Paul as being present when each of his letters was written with the coming and going of the 'we' of *Acts*, combined with the assumption that the author cannot have been any of those individuals actually named in *Acts*. In particular, 2 Tim. 4.11 ('Luke alone is with me') may have been a decisive passage in suggesting the identification, since the 'we' seems to have been present at Paul's arrival in Rome at the end of *Acts*. That the author was a doctor would then follow from Col. 4.14. There seems to be no other reason for believing that the author of *Acts* had a medical background. Claims that medical knowledge, or specialised medical vocabulary, can be found in *Acts* (see especially A. Harnack, *Luke the Physician*) were definitively refuted by H.J. Cadbury (*Style and Literary Method of Luke*, Harvard Theological Studies vi, 1919 and 1920), who demonstrated that the author of *Acts* shows no greater familiarity with medical terms and concepts than other non-medical writers. The association of Luke with Antioch may be based on nothing more than the fact that the author of *Acts* seems to have a special interest in, and knowledge of, events in Antioch (e.g. 11.19-30).

If it is the case that the traditional identification of the author of *Acts* with the Luke of Paul's letters rests, not on an independent tradition, but on evidence derived from *Acts* itself, then it is clear that statements of the traditional view in ancient authors are valuable only in so far as they demonstrate that no alternative tradition existed to challenge it.

There is, unfortunately, very little independent evidence for either the authorship or the date of *Acts* which would help us decide whether the traditional view is tenable. The earliest certain references to the work are in Irenaeus (*Adv. Haer.* 3, 14, 1) and in Clement of Alexandria (*Strom.* 5, 12; *Adumb. in 1 Petr.*) both late in the 2nd century. Attempts to find echoes or reminiscences of *Acts* in earlier authors are not entirely convincing, since there is no way of demonstrating that similarities of vocabulary, expression, or ideas arise from dependence on *Acts* itself, rather than on the tradition on which *Acts* itself relies. It would seem reasonable to assume, however, that since both Irenaeus and Clement believed *Acts* to have been written by a companion of Paul, it was a familiar work by the middle of the 2nd century. On the other hand, the most securely dateable event in *Acts*, Gallio's proconsulship of Achaea, is probably to be placed in 51-2, which enables us to calculate that the last event mentioned in *Acts*, the end of the two-year period which Paul spent in Rome, can be no later than 62. So we can say with reasonable certainty that *Acts* must have been published sometime between 62 and the middle of the second century. Before attempting to go further than this, it is necessary to consider four puzzling aspects of *Acts* which have a bearing on the question of who wrote the work, and when. They are: (1) the conclusion of *Acts*; (2) the relationship of *Acts* to the Gospel of Luke and its date; (3) the relationship of *Acts* to the letters of Paul; (4) the 'we' passages.

The conclusion of Acts

The last chapter brings Paul to Rome. He has been arrested in Jerusalem, and charges of disturbing the peace have been brought against him. Eventually he appeals to Caesar, and is transferred to Rome. The reader anticipates a trial and a verdict, or at least some indication of how the matter turned out. In fact, we are told nothing. The work ends with the simple statement that Paul stayed at Rome for two years, preaching unhindered. There are only two possible explanations of the author's failure to tell us what happened next: (i) that he knew no more; (ii) that he knew, but chose not to tell us.

Since it is surely inconceivable that Paul's subsequent history was known, but that the author of *Acts* could discover nothing about it, explanation (i) implies that there was nothing more to know. That is to say, the composition of *Acts* was completed two years after Paul's arrival at Rome, and the last verse of the last chapter brings us up to date with the situation at the time that the work was made public. There are some difficulties with this explanation. The ending remains strangely abrupt. Some phrase indicating that this was the present situation might have been expected. Besides, why would the author choose that time to issue what was in effect an incomplete story? What was the pressing need to publish in such a hurry? The date for the composition of *Acts* which this approach suggests (before 62) is very early, and, if it is accepted, will have implications for the date of composition of (for example) the gospels. If there is an allusion to Paul's own death in his speech to the Ephesian elders (see notes on 20.25), then explanation (i) is ruled out.

Explanation (ii), that the author knew more, but chose not to tell us, raises the problem of why he chose not to tell us. If the accusations against

Paul failed, either by an acquittal or by default, the author would have every reason to tell us, since it would fit well with his claim that Roman officials always found that the Jews' accusations against Paul and the other Christians were groundless. If, on the other hand, Paul had been condemned and punished, he can hardly have hoped to conceal the fact. The traditional view in the early church was that Paul was not killed at this point, but survived to carry out further missionary work (1 Tim. 4.16), perhaps including his visit to Spain announced at Rom. 15.28 (of which the reference to 'reaching the limit of the West' in 1 Clement 5.6 is perhaps a reflection), and was martyred during Nero's persecution in 64 (Eusebius, *Ecclesiastical History* 2, 22). It is just possible that the original ending of *Acts* was lost at some stage because it ended with Paul's condemnation and death, and so conflicted with the tradition. Otherwise, we must argue that *Acts* ends where it does because it suits the author's purpose; that he omits Paul's execution because it does not fit in with the picture he wishes to give us of good relations between the Romans and the Christians; or that Paul's martyrdom was so well known that he did not feel it necessary to include it; or (perhaps less implausibly) that he felt the preaching of the gospel at Rome, the centre of the empire, to be the culmination of Paul's work, and so the natural ending to the book; or that he intended to complete the story in a third book, which was either not written, or has vanished without trace.

The relationship to the gospel of Luke

The first two verses of *Acts* allude to a previous work dealing with the acts of Jesus, and are addressed to one Theophilus. Since the preface to the Gospel of Luke is also addressed to a Theophilus, there can be no doubt that we are intended to assume that it is the previous work which *Acts* follows. There is no reason to disbelieve this claim. But if *Acts* is a sequel to the Gospel of Luke, then the dating of the Gospel will be relevant to the dating of *Acts*. It is frequently argued that the prophecies of the fall of Jerusalem which the Synoptic Gospels contain are evidence that they were composed after the Jewish revolt, and the Roman capture of the city in 70 (for a contrary view, see especially J.A.T. Robinson, *Redating the New Testament*). This argument has particular force in the case of the Gospel of Luke. There is general agreement that one of the sources used in the composition of *Luke* was the Gospel of Mark (or possibly Matthew). When we compare the prophecy of the fall of Jerusalem in *Mark* and *Matthew* with the corresponding passage in *Luke*, it is hard to escape the conclusion that the prophecy has been re-written in the light of its actual fulfilment:

Mark 13.14, 19: But when you see the desolating sacrilege set up where it ought not to be (let the reader understand) then let those who are in Judaea flee to the mountains.... For in those days there will be such tribulation as has not been from the beginning of the creation which God created until now, no, and never will be.

Matthew 24, 15-16, 21: So when you see the desolating sacrilege spoken of by the prophet Daniel, standing in the holy place (let the reader understand), then let those who are in Judaea flee to the mountains.... For then there will be a great tribulation, such as has not been from the beginning of the world until now, no, and never will be.

Luke 21.20-1, 25: But when you see Jerusalem surrounded by armies, then know that its desolation has come near. Then let those that are in Judaea flee to the mountains, and let those who are inside the city depart, and let not those who are out in the country enter it.... They will fall by the edge of the sword, and be led captive among all nations; and Jerusalem will be trodden down by the Gentiles....

If this argument is accepted, then *Acts*, like *Luke*, must have been composed after 70 (unless we accept the view that the work which preceded *Acts* was not the Gospel of Luke which we now have, but a hypothetical 'proto-Luke', which was subsequently revised to include, among other things, the 'harder' form of the prophecy of the fall of Jerusalem). If we go further, and accept that *Mark* and *Matthew* were composed after 70, *Luke* and *Acts* must be placed later still. The preface to *Luke* makes it clear that it was not the first gospel to be written (*Luke* 1.1), and this is confirmed by clear signs that either *Mark* or *Matthew* was used as a source in the composition of *Luke*. It is perhaps surprising that *Acts*, which pays so much attention to the question of whether Gentiles must become Jews before they can become Christians, does not contain clearer allusions to the fall of Jerusalem and the destruction of the Temple if these events had already occurred at the time of composition. On the other hand, even works which were manifestly written after 70 refer to the fall of Jerusalem much less frequently than we would expect. The Epistle of Barnabas, for example, which deals extensively with the rival claims of Jews and Christians, mentions the fall of Jerusalem only once (16.4-5), and then only in the context of a discussion of the Temple. So the fact that *Acts* does not contain allusions to the events of 70 is not necessarily an indication that it cannot have been composed after 70.

Acts *and the letters of Paul*

The question whether the picture of Paul given in *Acts* is compatible with what Paul reveals of himself in his letters, and whether the account of the events of Paul's life given in *Acts* can be reconciled with what we are told in the letters has been hotly debated. Clearly, if there are substantial discrepancies between *Acts* and Paul's own account, the possibility that *Acts* was written by someone who knew Paul personally is greatly reduced. *Acts* has been subject to criticism on the grounds that: (a) it shows no knowledge of Paul's theology; and (b) the account of events which it gives is inconsistent with what Paul himself says.

a) *Theology*. No-one with experience of teaching will find it remarkable if a pupil, even an intelligent and conscientious one, is found to misrepresent or misunderstand his master's views. The fact that Paul's distinctive theology is, in general, absent from *Acts* is not in itself a proof that the author was not a member of Paul's circle. *Acts* is not a work which goes in much for theological argument, beyond what is necessary for the narrative, and we should not expect to find anything like a full exposition of Pauline theology. It is nevertheless a little odd that Paul's most distinctive teaching, that the Law leads to sin (Gal. 3.19; Rom. 4.13-16; 1 Cor. 15.56; 2 Cor. 3.6), is not found anywhere in his account of his dispute with those who wished to impose the Jewish Law on Gentile converts. It is also odd that Paul's emphatic claim to be an apostle is not reflected in *Acts* (see above p. 2). More serious, however, is the claim that *Acts* represents Paul as doing things which the author of the Epistles could not consistently have done. In 16.1-3 Paul is represented as having Timothy, son of a Jewish mother and a Greek father, circumcised at Lystra (or Derbe) before he accepts him as a companion. In *Galatians* (perhaps addressed to the churches at Lystra and Derbe, among others) Paul belabours the point that circumcision was not merely superfluous, but that 'if you get yourselves circumcised, Christ will be of no help to you at all' (Gal. 5.2). Emerson may have dismissed consistency as 'the hobgoblin of little minds' (quoted by Bruce, p. 58), but the recipients of *Galatians* would surely be entitled to be startled by the circumcision of Timothy. Similarly, Paul's vow at 18.18 has been felt by some to be inconsistent with the doctrine of Grace found in the Epistles. Another recurrent feature of the narrative of *Acts*, which has been held to be inconsistent with the emphasis in the Epistles on Paul's mission to the Gentiles (esp. Gal. 2.9), is his teaching in the synagogue or its equivalent in each city (13.5 Salamis; 13.14 Antioch; 14.1 Iconium; 16.13 Philippi; 17.1-2 Thessalonica; 17.10 Beroea; 17.17 Athens; 18.4

Corinth; 18.19 Ephesus; for the argument, see W.A. Meeks, *The First Urban Christians*, p. 26). However, it would make very good sense for a Christian missionary to the Gentiles to visit the synagogues first because it is there that he could find those Gentiles, the 'god-fearers' (see p. 21), who would best be able to understand what he was talking about. Paul's mention among his sufferings (2 Cor. 11.24) of five floggings at the hands of the Jews tends to confirm that some of his work was carried out in synagogues.

b) *Inconsistencies in the narrative*. It is clear that *Acts* does not give us a full narrative of everything which happened to Paul during the period that it covers. Perhaps it is the author's intention to give us only a representative sample of events, rather than a full history (see p. 2 above). There are also indications that more could have been said about some of the episodes which are covered in *Acts*. For example, in 1 Cor. 15.32 Paul says: 'I fought with wild beasts at Ephesus' (presumably metaphorically – those who literally faced the wild beasts in the arena did not survive to write letters about it; in any case, as a Roman citizen Paul would not have been liable, at any rate legally, to be condemned to death by wild beasts, nor is it certain that this element in Roman *ludi* had been introduced into the Greek East as early as this); in 2 Cor. 1.8 he refers to a grave affliction he experienced 'in Asia', but *Acts*' account of the riot at Ephesus, in which Paul was *not* in any case personally involved, hardly matches the strength of Paul's own language. Either some major episode has been omitted (it has been held by some scholars that Paul was imprisoned) or the course of the riot has been seriously misrepresented. Similarly, Paul's letters to the Corinthians reveal that his relationship with the community there was much more complex and eventful than *Acts* would lead us to believe. Omissions of this kind may not be especially significant, and probably are to be accounted for by the author's exercise of his discretion to 'edit' the narrative so as to keep the work to a reasonable size (and perhaps also to play down episodes which reveal divisions in the church or conflicts with authority). More serious issues are raised when the account of an episode given by *Acts* is substantially different from that given by Paul himself. The main focus of criticism in this area has been Paul's own account of his career in *Galatians* 1-2. This letter mentions only two visits by Paul to Jerusalem after his conversion (Gal. 1.18, 2.1) while *Acts* records three such visits (9.26; 11.30 and 12.25; 15.2-30); and there are serious problems in reconciling the description of the 'Council at Jerusalem' in *Acts* 15 with Paul's account of his meeting with the 'pillars' of the church at Jerusalem in *Galatians* 2. A possible solution to some of these difficulties (but one which is unacceptable to many biblical scholars) is to argue that the epistle was addressed to the churches at Antioch, Iconium, Lystra, and Derbe, after Paul's first missionary journey, but before the third visit to Jerusalem recorded in *Acts* 15; in that case the second visit of *Galatians* 2 would be the same as the second visit of *Acts* 11.30 and 12.25, of which *Acts* gives hardly any details (see F.F. Bruce, *Bull. J. Ryl. Lib.* 54, pp. 250-67). Even if we accept this view, however, serious difficulties remain. The root of the problem lies in the different purposes of each writer. *Acts*, as always, wishes to emphasise the unity of the church, so that Paul is represented as accepting the authority of the apostles at Jerusalem; he refers difficult questions to them (15.2); the dispute about the admission of Gentiles is settled by an amicable (and authoritative) agreement (15.13-33). Paul, on the other hand, wishes to emphasise his own independent authority. He has received his gospel not from men, but by revelation from Christ himself (Gal. 1.1); it was three years after his conversion before he went to Jerusalem (Gal. 1.17-18); he does not derive his authority from Peter or James or John or any other man, but from God himself. It is very difficult to reconcile these two pictures. What is more, it is hard to explain why, if an authoritative statement of the conditions under which Gentiles could be admitted to the church was agreed at Jerusalem, no hint of any kind of the existence of such an agreement should be found in any of Paul's writings.

Discrepancies of this kind do not rule out the possibility that *Acts* was written by an associate and companion of Paul. Indeed, the picture we are given of Paul in *Acts* is certainly no more different from the Paul of the Epistles than Xenophon's picture of Socrates is different from that of Plato. Nevertheless, they do make it more difficult to accept that the work was completed before, or very shortly after, Paul's death.

There is one firm conclusion which can be drawn from the comparison of *Acts* with Paul's Epistles. The author of *Acts* cannot have used the collection of letters which we now have as one of his sources. Had he done so, it is inconceivable that he would not have attempted to eliminate or explain away the inconsistencies. Obviously, from the time that it was written, each letter would have been available locally to the church to which it had been sent, and to others to whom it had been passed on, but it seems to have been some time before the letters were collected together and made universally available. The author of 1 Clement (perhaps writing in Rome at the end of the 1st century) knows *Romans* (35, 6), *1 Corinthians* (e.g. 47, 1-3), and perhaps others as well. Ignatius, at the beginning of the 2nd century, clearly knows a number of Pauline letters (*Letter to the Ephesians* 12, 2). It is clear, then, that the corpus of Paul's letters was well on the way to being formed by the beginning of the 2nd century, so it is probable that *Acts* had been written before that date.

The 'we' passages

Perhaps the most puzzling feature of *Acts* is the unexplained introduction into the narrative of a number of passages in the first person plural – the 'we' passages. The first 'we' is found at 16.10, when Paul and his companions, in response to a vision sent to Paul, decide to travel to Macedonia. The 'we' remains during the voyage to Philippi, the conversion of Lydia, and the casting out of a spirit from a slave girl. When Paul and Silas are arrested and imprisoned (16.19) the 'we' is absent, and when the journey resumes (17.1) the narrative continues in the third person. The 'we' returns at 20.5 when Paul takes ship from Philippi to Troas, where it remains with him during the raising of Eutychus from the dead. The 'we' then, *without* Paul, sails to Assos, where Paul is taken on board, and they travel together to Mitylene, and from there to Miletus. During Paul's address to the elders at Ephesus the 'we' is naturally absent, but it is there when they set sail again (21.1), and present throughout the journey to Jerusalem, as far as the reception of Paul and his companions by the Jerusalem church, and the meeting with James and the elders (21.18). From 21.19 to 26.32 the narrative is centred very much on Paul himself (indeed for much of it he is on trial or in prison). The 'we' is absent, probably because there is nowhere in the narrative where it could be naturally introduced. When Paul leaves prison to travel to Rome (27.1) the 'we' is there again, and remains to the end of the book. (One group of manuscripts, the so-called 'Western' text, has an additional 'we' at 11.28.)

We are offered no explanation for the introduction of these first-person narratives. They begin abruptly. We are never told who the first-person narrator is. The events described are no different from those described in the rest of the book. There is no increase in detail or graphic description. There are no claims on the part of the narrator to have been an eye-witness to startling or momentous events. Much of these narratives is concerned with travel, but they are not 'travel narratives'. Preaching, healing, exhortation, sufferings, and tribulation are found in these sections no less than in the rest of *Acts*.

There seems to be no other ancient historical work which mixes first- and third-person narratives quite in this way. The normal convention among ancient historians was to write in the third person, even when they themselves had been involved either in the whole of the action (e.g. Xenophon's *Anabasis*, Caesar's *Gallic War*), or in a particular episode (e.g. Thucydides 4, 104, 4 – 106, 4). However, although a historian will refer to himself as a *participant* in the action in the third person, when he speaks to his readers as *author* he will often use the first. For example, where there is a preface it is usually in the first person (e.g. Thucydides 1, 22 and 5, 25, 4-6; Tacitus, *Annals* 1, 1; the prefaces to *Luke* and *Acts* are of this kind); an author may make personal observations in the first person (e.g. Caesar, *Gallic War* 5, 13, 4; Tacitus, *Annals* 11, 11); he may speak in the first person to make a claim to have been an eye-witness to a particular event (e.g. Velleius Paterculus 2, 101, 3; Dio Cassius 73, 7, 1 and 74, 12, 1-4). None of this, however, is of any help with the 'we' passages of *Acts*. Given that the normal convention is to use the third person in narratives, the occasional uses of the first person by a historian are natural and explicable. There is no mystery about them. The author is stepping out of the narrative to address us directly. But there is nothing in the work of other ancient historians comparable to the way in which *Acts* slips into and out of the first person without explanation.

Nor are there clear precedents in Jewish writers. The historical books of the Old Testament are, in general, simple third person narratives. *Tobit* begins with a long passage in the first person, and moves into the third person for the substance of the story, but this is quite different from what we find in *Acts*. The only book in the Old Testament which contains anything comparable to the 'we' passages of *Acts* is *Ezra/Nehemiah*. (*Ezra* and *Nehemiah* originally formed a single book; although it was divided into two in the Greek version as early as Origen in the 3rd century, in the Hebrew text the division did not occur until 1448; there is general agreement that the book is in fact a continuation of *Chronicles*). *Ezra/Nehemiah* begins in the third person, moves to a first person narrative by Ezra (Ezra 7.28-9.15) and then continues in the third person until a first person narrative by Nehemiah is introduced (Neh. 1.1-7.5). A final first person narrative is introduced at Neh. 12.31. There is, however, no difficulty in explaining the use of first and third persons in this book. *Ezra/Nehemiah* is transparently a work which consists largely of extracts from other documents. It is quite clear that the sections in the first person are simply extended quotations from earlier works. There is no attempt to edit them or integrate them into the general narrative. The 'we' passages of *Acts* are quite different. Although the introduction of the 'we' is unexpected, the narrative runs smoothly. The language and style of the 'we' passages is indistinguishable from that of the rest of the book. There is no indication that the 'we' passages are extracts or quotations from an existing work which have been introduced into *Acts*.

There is, then, no precedent for the 'we' passages of *Acts* in the works of other writers, and the author of *Acts* is not following any generally understood literary or historical convention.

Unless we take the view that the author is following some convention otherwise unknown (such as a hypothetical convention that travel narratives are in the first person), there are two ways of explaining the 'we' passages: (i) the author wishes to show that he was present on those occasions where the narrative is in the first person; (ii) the 'we' is carried over into *Acts* from another document, one of the sources used in the composition of *Acts*.

The problem with explanations of the first kind is that the simple use of the first person is not a recognised method, which the author could be sure that his readers would understand, of making it clear that the author is claiming to have been present at the time. When ancient authors want their readers to know that they were present at particular occasions, they usually tell them so (e.g. Velleius Paterculus 2, 101, 1-3: *quod spectaculum... tribuno militum mihi visere contigit*, 'I witnessed this sight as a military tribune'). Even in the apocryphal Acts of various apostles, which were written from the 2nd century onwards in imitation of *Acts*, where a first-person narrator occurs he is presented much more explicitly as a witness of, and participant in, the events (see for example *Acts of John* 60-1, where the apostle banishes the bed-bugs from an inn where he was staying: 'Now as the day was breaking I got up first, and Verus and Andronicus with me; and we saw by the door of the room which we had taken a mass of bugs collected.... We were astounded at the great number of them.... We explained to (John) what we had seen.... And he sat up in bed and looked at them and said, "Since you have behaved yourselves,...go to your own place." And when he had said this the bugs came running from the door towards the bed and climbed up its legs and disappeared into the joints.'). The probability is that the 'we' passages of *Acts* would have been as mysterious to readers in the 1st century as they are to us. If *Acts* had been written for a particular community, by a member of that community, known to all of them, it is possible that the use of 'we' would have been understood as a claim (of which the community would already be aware) that the author had been a companion of Paul. But once the work got beyond the author's immediate circle, the significance of the 'we' passages would no longer be clear. It is hard to envisage circumstances in which the author of *Acts* would write a work of this kind, without intending that it should be circulated beyond his own immediate acquaintances. But what does seem to be ruled out is the possibility that the 'we' passages were inserted into *Acts* by an author who was not a companion of Paul, but who wished to give his work a spurious authority. Such an author would surely have chosen a much more unambiguous and straightforward way of claiming the authority of an eyewitness (as the authors of the apocryphal Acts do).

The second kind of explanation, that the 'we' has survived from an earlier document, which was written in the first person, and which was used as a source for *Acts*, raises its own problems. The author of *Acts* was not a simple compiler of source material. He re-shapes and re-writes his material with great confidence and skill, as we can see in the way he re-works *Mark* (or *Matthew*) in composing *Luke*. But even the most dull and incompetent writer must be capable of recognising a 'we' and changing it into a 'they'. The 'we' passages do not appear to be in any way intrusions into the narrative, nor are they stylistically or linguistically distinct from the rest of *Acts*. It is difficult to escape the conclusion that the 'we' passages are the compositions of the author in the same way that the rest of *Acts* is, and that the 'we's are there because he wants them to be there, because they have some significance. It is perhaps possible that the author wished to let us know that for certain episodes he had first-hand evidence, the account, either written or oral, of one of Paul's companions, and, following *Ezra/Nehemiah* as a model, believed that the retention of the first person was the proper way of indicating this.

The truth is that there is no explanation of the 'we' passages which does not leave as many problems as it solves. 'They are a remarkably difficult phenomenon, and their interpretation depends on, and does not solve, the problem of the authorship of *Acts*' (BC II, pp. 160-1).

Conclusions

The fact that the author of *Acts* clearly could not have used Paul's letters as a source points to a date of composition in the 1st century (or at any rate no later than the very beginning of the 2nd century). If we accept the argument that *Luke*, and therefore *Acts*, must have been written after the fall of Jerusalem, then a date in the 80s or 90s looks as likely as any. Such a date would certainly not rule out the possibility that the author was a companion of Paul, but the 'we' passages do not compel us to believe that he was, and, unless the tradition repeated by early Christian writers rests on evidence more substantial than inferences drawn from *Acts* itself (and there is no reason to believe that it does), it must remain a possibility rather than a probability. Beyond that we cannot go.

III The historical context of *Acts*

A: *The cities* (poleis) *of the eastern Roman empire*

Paul's missionary efforts, described from *Acts* 13 onwards, involved visits to a number of self-governing communities (Latin *civitates*, Greek *poleis*) in the subject provinces of the Roman empire. The life of these communities can be reconstructed with the aid of surviving works of Greek and Latin literature, and of the inscriptions, coins, and physical remains of the cities themselves. The following aspects of the cities' institutions will be considered here: (1) status; (2) internal government; (3) urban disorder; (4) town and countryside; (5) citizens and resident aliens.

1) Status. The cities of the eastern provinces can be divided into three categories: (a) Roman *coloniae*; (b) subject cities with privileges; (c) subject cities without privileges.

a) Roman *coloniae.* (Of the places visited by Paul, the following were *coloniae*: Pisidian Antioch, Iconium, Lystra, Troas, Philippi, Corinth.) It had been the Romans' practice from the earliest stages of their conquests in Italy to confiscate land from their defeated enemies and use it to provide farms for their own citizens; such settler-farmers (*coloni*) were often organised into a new self-governing city with its own urban centre (a *colonia*). In the later part of the 1st century BC such 'colonies' were founded in the provinces on land expropriated or bought from the native population. The *coloni* were in most cases veteran soldiers from the Roman legions, and the farms allotted to them were their reward for their services to the state; Corinth was an exception, since it had been planned by Julius Caesar to provide for the urban poor of Rome itself. Many provincial *coloniae* also served the strategic function of placing ex-soldiers where they could keep watch over potentially troublesome subject peoples; Pisidian Antioch, Iconium, and Lystra belonged to a group of nine such colonies planted by Augustus in the province of Galatia (see B. Levick, *Roman Colonies in Southern Asia Minor*, ch. 4; but with the modifications made by S. Mitchell, *Historia* 28 [1979] 409-38).

In the eastern provinces the colonists used as their urban centre an existing town (Roman Corinth was built on the deserted site of the old Greek city destroyed by Rome in 146 BC) and the old name was usually incorporated into the formal Latin title of the colony and survived as the everyday name of the place. What happened to the original native communities is uncertain; in only a few cases was such a *polis* allowed to continue in existence on the same site as part of a 'double community' (it is now known that such was the situation at Iconium from the time of Augustus: see Mitchell op. cit.). In the eastern provinces, where Greek was the *lingua franca*, Greek soon became the everyday language of the descendants of the original colonists, although Latin was long kept in use for official purposes (Levick, op. cit., chs 11-12). The *coloni* (i.e. those with full citizenship in a particular *colonia*) would have been especially conscious of their status as Roman citizens (see B.4 below) in contrast to their neighbours in Greek *poleis*, who were foreigners (*peregrini*) in Roman eyes.

b) Subject cities with privileges. The natives of Roman provinces were officially described as 'allies and friends of the Roman people' (*socii et* *amici populi Romani*), but this did not in any way mitigate their tributary and subject status. In most provinces the self-governing communities (*civitates*) were permitted a great measure of internal autonomy, but under the supervision of the Roman governor. But a few such 'cities' enjoyed virtual immunity from intervention by the governors in their internal affairs; they were classed as *civitates liberae et foederatae* (free and allied cities, i.e. in possession of a treaty of alliance with Rome) or as *civitates liberae* (free cities, i.e. free in virtue of a unilateral grant by Rome). Two cities visited by Paul are known to have belonged to the second group, viz. Thessalonica and Athens.

c) **Subject cities without privileges.** The remaining cities visited by Paul were ordinary tributary cities (*civitates stipendariae*). It is remarkable how few of the cities actually evangelised by him did belong to this, the most numerous, category of provincial cities: Salamis in Cyprus (13.5), Derbe (14.21), Perge (14.25), Beroea (17.11-12), Ephesus (18.19, 19.1-20); and only Ephesus receives extended treatment from the author of *Acts*.

2) **The internal government of the cities.** The city-states of the Mediterranean world normally had three main organs of government: (i) an Assembly, which any citizen with full political rights could attend, and which elected the city magistrates (see iii) and voted on laws; (ii) a Council, which discussed proposals before the Assembly voted on them, and which supervised the work of the magistrates; (iii) Magistrates, the executive officers of the city, in most cases elected by the Assembly and replaced every year. Rome itself under the Republic had been governed jointly by three such organs: the voting assemblies known as *Comitia*; the Senate of 300 (later 600) members; and the colleges of annual magistrates, of which the two consuls were the most senior. Since Roman colonies were miniature copies of Rome itself, each one had *comitia* open to all *coloni*, an *ordo* of 100 *decuriones*, and three pairs of annual magistrates, the most senior of whom were the *duoviri iure dicundo* (= the *strategoi* of *Acts* 16.20). Greek *poleis* usually had an *ekklesia* (assembly) open to all citizens (19.32, 40), a *boule* (council) whose size and composition varied from *polis* to *polis*, and annual officials, for whom the generic term was *archontes* (applied to the *duoviri* of Philippi in 16.19), but whose numbers, titles, and functions also varied (e.g. *politarchai*, 'city leaders', at Thessalonica, 17.6; and the *grammateus tou demou*, 'clerk of the people' at Ephesus, 19.35). Athens, exceptionally, had two Councils: the Areopagus whose members served for life; and the Council of 600 which was replaced annually; the Areopagus seems to have carried out the functions performed by senior magistrates in other cities (see notes on 17.19).

Most Greek cities at the time they came under Roman rule still retained a considerable degree of effective democracy, with genuine decision-making by the Assemblies. By AD 200 this had been curbed and the Councils had become both the effective governing bodies in the cities and closed corporations recruited from a hereditary aristocracy of the landed gentry (see G.E.M. de Ste. Croix, *The Class Struggle in the Ancient Greek World*, pp. 518-37, for the fullest survey of this process). Sherwin-White (1963, pp. 174-5) held that the picture of city government given in *Acts* corresponded well with the state of affairs which still prevailed around AD 50 but had disappeared by AD 150: 'The stress in *Acts* is on the actual magistrates in office, and the mass of the population plays some part in affairs: the *demos* is active both at Ephesus and Thessalonica. The city councils, so predominant at the later period, are conspicuously absent from the story' (p. 175). Too much, however, should not be made of the facts cited by Sherwin-White: (a) it is not surprising that it was the magistrates and not the Councils who took action when a response to a sudden emergency was called for (especially at Thessalonica and Ephesus, and to a lesser degree at Philippi and Athens), since it was only the executive officers, and not deliberative bodies of at least 100 men which were not in permanent session, who could make such a response *at any period*; (b) only in *one* city, Ephesus, is there a reference to an *ekklesia* (the *demos* at Thessalonica was probably a mob; see note on 17.5), and it is far from clear that the meeting in the theatre at Ephesus was a properly constituted *ekklesia* (see note on 19.40), although it must be conceded that in 19.39 the Clerk of the People envisages a decision being reached in the *ekklesia* without any apparent discussion by the *boule*. It cannot therefore be demonstrated that *Acts*' picture of civic institutions reflects a situation which cannot have existed later than the 1st century AD.

3) Urban disorder. The preaching of Paul and/or his associates leads to public disturbances in no fewer than six cities: Pisidian Antioch (13.50); Iconium (14.5); Lystra (14.19); Thessalonica (17.5); Beroea (17.13); Ephesus (19.29). Likewise at Philippi the accusations against Paul and Silas 'provoke the crowd' (16.20), while at Corinth a man was beaten up in front of the proconsul's tribunal (18.17). The 'manufacture of a mob' is represented as a fairly easy matter, and our other sources confirm that *Acts* is 'true to life' in this respect.

The speeches of the Greek orator Dio Chrysostom, from Prusa in Bithynia, give a vivid picture of the activities of urban mobs around AD 100: 'What kind of human beings in their anger with their fellow citizens...do not give reasons or wait to hear reasons but at once throw stones or burn houses in order that, if possible, you might burn them up with their wives and children?' (*Oration* 46, 11). The emperor Augustus in a letter to the city of Knidos described the use of a mob in a private vendetta: 'I was informed that Philinus son of Chrysippus attacked the house of Eubulus and Tryphera for three nights on end with violence and a virtual siege; that on the third night his brother Eubulus joined in the assault; that Eubulus and Tryphera, the owners of the house, being unable to find safety in their own home, either by treating with Philinus or by barricading the house against the assaults, ordered one of their slaves, not indeed to kill (to which a man might perhaps be driven by a not unjustified anger), but to keep them away by showering them with excreta; but that the slave, whether by accident or design,…let go the pot along with the contents that were being poured down; and that Eubulus was struck down, although it would have been fairer had he survived instead of his brother' (for the Greek text, see R.K. Sherk, *Roman Documents from the Greek East* 67, ll. 13-27).

The underemployed urban poor (see 17.5) might be roused to demonstrate or to riot by the fear of hunger when the food supply of a town was interrupted; Dio of Prusa had been accused of hoarding grain to make a profit during a dearth (Or. 46, 8). Men employed in a particular trade might protest when their livelihood seemed to be threatened; not only the silversmiths, but also the bakers, of Ephesus (see notes on 19, 24-7). Unpopular 'alien' minorities might become the victims of mob violence, such as the Jews of Alexandria in the reign of Gaius, and those in cities in the neighbourhood of Judaea after the Jewish revolt of AD 66. A general resentment of the rich minority by the poor majority might lead to such acts as the burning down of the archives and public records (presumably including all IOUs and mortgages) at Dyme in Greece ca. 115 BC (Sherk, op. cit., no. 43; translated by Sherk, *Rome and the Greek East*, p. 54).

It was easy to 'manufacture mobs', and for demonstrations to turn into virtual rebellions because the city authorities had no police or gendarmerie at their disposal to suppress trouble in its early stages, and units of Roman soldiers were not usually stationed in 'peaceful' provinces such as Achaea or Asia. The Roman government was therefore anxious in case urban disorders got out of hand, and the local gentry who held executive offices in the cities, and whose monopoly of power was supported by Rome, were expected to see to it that they did not (hence the anxiety of the Clerk of the People at Ephesus in ch. 19). This is made clear by Plutarch in his *Political Precepts* addressed to young gentlemen on entering public life in their native cities (ca. AD 100); he compares the mob to a fractious animal which needs to be kept under control by the gentry through rhetorical skills (*Moralia* 800C, 802D, 814C, 821A, 823E-F). Plutarch also expresses the fear that rivalries between leading families might lead some aristocrats to use mobs to injure their rivals (*Moralia* 825A-D, 818C). In Dio's native province of Bithynia such faction fights had become such a problem by ca. AD 100 that the Roman governor Pliny was instructed by the emperor Trajan to ban meetings by associations of any kind, and Trajan refused to make an exception even for voluntary fire-fighters: 'whatever name, for whatever cause, we may give to those who associate for the same purpose, they will soon turn into political cliques' (Pliny, *Epistles* 10, 34).

4) Town and countryside. The conventional translation of *civitas/polis* as 'city' is misleading in view of the fact that the most usual meaning of the word in English is 'large town'. A *civitas* was a self-governing community, a body of citizens living in a demarcated territory. In most *poleis* in classical Greece there was, it is true, a walled town which served as the political, religious, and economic focus of the territory; but the 'city-state' called Athens in English was officially known as *hoi Athenaioi*, 'the Athenians', a term which covered the residents of the countryside of Attica as well as of the town of Athens.

However, G.E.M. de Ste. Croix has pointed out that a different state of affairs prevailed outside the homeland of the Greeks, in the interior of Asia Minor and in Syria, where native towns had become Hellenised, and new *poleis* had been founded by kings in the centuries following Alexander's conquest of the Persian Empire. In those regions a great cultural and linguistic gulf separated the world of the *polis* from that of the *chora*, the countryside, and the Greek-speaking urban populations from the surrounding peasantry speaking their ancestral vernaculars (e.g. Phrygian and Lycaonian in the interior of Asia Minor; cf. 14.11). Hence there is a contrast between Jesus' mission among the rural Jews of Galilee and Paul's among the urban 'Hellenes and Jews' of Asia Minor and Greece (G.E.M. de Ste. Croix in *Studies in Church History*, vol. 12 [1975], D. Baker [ed.], pp. 1-38, and *The Class Struggle*, pp. 9-19, 427-30; see also W.A. Meeks, *The First Urban Christians*, pp. 9-16).

Paul's mission in *Acts* is confined almost wholly to the towns (a possible exception is 'the country round Lystra and Derbe': see note on 14.6). De Ste. Croix shows that the linguistic and cultural division between *polis* and *chora* explains this restriction in the interior of Asia Minor, but it also affected Paul in areas where Greek was the language of the countryside as well as of the towns (Cyprus, Macedonia, Achaea, and the west coast of Asia Minor). Presumably it would be far harder for a stranger preaching a strange doctrine, and himself an urban craftsman (18.3), to get a hearing from farmers working their ancestral lands than from the mixed populations of the towns. (On relationships between town and country in general in this period, see Ramsay MacMullen, *Roman Social Relations*, chs 1-2.)

5) Citizens and resident aliens. The chief criterion for citizenship in a classical Greek *polis* was not residence or place of birth but ancestry; the principle was applied most rigorously in democratic Athens, where citizens had to be of citizen descent on both sides, and a grant of citizenship to an individual foreigner required a vote of the *ekklesia*, ratified at a subsequent meeting with a quorum of 6,000. At the same time Athens permitted and even encouraged large-scale immigration of foreign craftsmen, traders, and financiers; they and their descendants remained resident aliens. There is thus a striking contrast between classical states, which allowed unrestricted immigration but rarely 'naturalised' resident aliens, and modern states which limit immigration for settlement but usually allow the naturalisation of most permanent residents.

This pattern continued to apply to the 'cities' of the Roman period; the classical Roman jurists discuss the claims which can be made on a man by his *domicilium* (city of residence) and by his *origo* (the city, not necessarily of his own birth, but from which his ancestors sprang). As a result the populations of the towns Paul visited would be of mixed background and religious affiliation, although they would have Greek as a *lingua franca*. Craftsmen and traders migrated freely; the Gentile Lydia, who had moved from Thyateira to Philippi (16.14), and the Jew Aquila, who must have gone from Pontus to Rome before coming to Corinth (18.2), are both characteristic figures. In the Roman colonies especially, the residents who were full citizens were probably a minority (Sherwin-White [1963] p. 177).

One category of resident foreigners met with special difficulties, the Jews (their presence in many towns throughout the eastern provinces is attested by inscriptions, papyri, and Josephus); their export of money to support the Temple at Jerusalem, for example, was resented. Documents preserved by Josephus show Roman authorities intervening to protect Jews from harassment at the hands of city authorities (T. Rajak, *Journal of Roman Studies* 74 [1984] pp. 107-23). It appears from *Acts* that the Jewish synagogues in the cities attracted the interest of numbers of Gentiles, especially women, who worshipped the Jewish God; *Acts* refers to them as *phoboumenoi* or *sebomenoi ton theon* 'those who fear God' (Josephus describes Poppaea, Nero's second wife, as *theosebes* 'god-fearing': *Ant.* 20, 195). An inscription from Aphrodisias in the province of Asia lists the names of members of a synagogue, and the term *theosebeis* is used as a heading for a distinct group (J. Reynolds and R. Tannenbaum, *Jews and Godfearers at Aphrodisias*; see also Schürer² III [1] pp. 25-6): it shows that in one place at least the Jews themselves recognised the existence of 'god-fearers' as a group. One might speculate that it was the immigrant Gentile population of the cities, divorced from the public life of their places of residence and without ancestral ties to the local civic cults, who showed a special interest both in Judaism and in Pauline Christianity. (See in general Schürer² III [1] pp. 165-9.)

B: Roman government in the eastern provinces

In *Acts* Paul and his companions have far less contact with the representatives of the Roman imperial government outside Judaea (only at Paphos, 13.7-12, and at Corinth, 18.12-17) than they have with the local authorities in the cities, while the emperor likewise is mentioned only twice before Paul's final return to Judaea (17.6, 18.2). At Philippi Paul's own status as a Roman citizen is mentioned for the first time (16.37), and in the later chapters it becomes central to the narrative (22-7). The following subjects will be discussed here: (1) the emperor; (2) Roman provinces; (3) the provincial governors; (4) Roman citizens in the provinces.

1) The emperor. At Thessalonica the Christians are charged with acting in violation of the decrees of 'Caesar' (17.7); in 18.2 there is a reference to the ruling emperor, Claudius, by name. The fact that in Greek the only way one could refer to the real ruler of the Roman world was, not by a title (such as *basileus* [literally = 'king'] – which could be used of a false claimant to be a ruler, 17.7), but by a proper noun which was part of a Roman family name, Caesar, indicates the curious nature of the kind of monarchy founded by Augustus after the end of the civil wars; in theory the traditional Republican form of government continued, while a succession of individuals were vested with a range of 'extraordinary' powers. Hence there was in principle no *office* of emperor, and what happened in 27 BC – AD 41 was that three members of the same family (the Julius Caesar family) had exercised these 'special powers'. The accession of Claudius in AD 41 marks the start of a tradition whereby 'Caesar' became a title rather than a personal name (as a title it was to have a long history, with two Kaisers and two Tsars reigning in Europe in 1914). Tiberius Claudius Germanicus became 'emperor' after the murder of his nephew Gaius in 41, thanks to the support of the rank and file of the Praetorian Guards; unlike Gaius, or his uncle Tiberius, Claudius had never been adopted into the Julian family, but he added Caesar to his names anyway. All this should help to show that the position of the 'Caesars' resembled that of the Somoza or Duvallier families far more closely than that of the Hapsburgs or of the Bourbons.

As 18.2 indicates, Claudius closely supervised the administration of the city of Rome; on one day, while holding the office of censor, he issued twenty edicts, one of which offered unsolicited medical advice on antidotes to the venom of snakes (Suetonius, *Claudius* 16, 4). For practical reasons the Caesars could not become so deeply involved in the routine administration of the provinces; on the whole they did not try to impose 'policies' on the whole empire, but dealt with particular problems presented to them by governors, cities, or private individuals, to whom they were expected to keep themselves accessible (see F. Millar, *The Emperor in the Roman World*). An emperor resembled a universal ombudsman more than a modern President or Prime Minister.

2) Roman provinces and historical geography. During his journeys Paul visited eight different Roman provinces (see the list below), and he was prevented from entering a ninth province, Bithynia-Pontus (16.7). The territorial provinces of the Roman empire often comprised a variety of districts and peoples with distinct histories (e.g. the full title of a governor of Galatia is given in one inscription as 'of Galatia, of Pisidia, of Phrygia, of Lycaonia, of Isauria, of Paphlagonia, of Pontus Galaticus, of Pontus Polemoniacus, of Armenia': Dessau, no. 1017). Their frontiers also cut across ethnic and linguistic boundaries, especially in Asia Minor (e.g. Phrygia was divided between the provinces of Asia and Galatia [see notes on 16.6 and 18.23], and Lycaonia (14.6) between Galatia and the client kingdom of Antiochus IV of Commagene). The following languages, in addition to Greek, had been spoken in southern and western Asia Minor not long before Paul's travels: Cilician, Pamphylian, Lycaonian, Pisidian, Phrygian, Mysian, and Celtic. Provincial boundaries might be rearranged from time to time: the region of Pamphylia which Paul visited on his first journey (13.13, 14.24) had only recently (AD 43) been detached from the province of Galatia and linked to the previously 'free' republic of Lycia to form a new province, Lycia-Pamphylia (Levick, *Roman Colonies* 163). The Latin word *provincia* originally referred to the 'job' allotted (literally, by lot) to a consul or praetor in Republican Rome; the first use of geographical names to define 'provinces' came when consuls or praetors were sent to fight wars in areas such as Spain, Africa, or Macedonia; when wars resulted in annexations the first territorial provinces were organised, but the concept of a magistrate's *provincia* remained a highly flexible one.

The provinces (apart from Judaea), regions within provinces, and cities mentioned during Paul's missionary journeys are as follows:

	PROVINCES	CITIES	REGIONS
13.4	Cyprus	Salamis, Paphos	
13.13	Lycia-Pamphylia	Perge, Attaleia	Pamphylia (13.13, 14.24)

16.6	Galatia	Lystra, Derbe	Lycaonia (14.6; the eastern part was ruled by King Antiochus IV of Commagene), Pisidia (14.24)
		Antioch, Iconium	Phrygia (16.6, 18.23; part lay in the province of Asia)
15.23, 41	Syria	Antioch, Seleucia	Phoenicia (15.3), Cilicia (15.23, 41)
16.7	Bithynia (the western part of Bithynia-Pontus)		
16.6, 19.10, 22, 26-7	Asia	Troas, Assos Ephesus, Miletus, Mitylene, Samos	Mysia (16.7-8)
16.9-12, 18.5, 19.21-2, 20.1-3	Macedonia	Neapolis, Philippi, Amphipolis, Apollonia, Thessalonica, Beroea	The first *meris* of Macedonia (16.12)
18.12, 18.27, 19.21	Achaea	Athens, Corinth	Hellas (20.2) must refer to the province of Achaea

3) Roman governors. The two governors whom Paul encountered outside Judaea both had the title proconsul (*anthupatos*: 13.7, 8, 12; 18.12) and the same title was borne by the governors of Asia referred to at Ephesus (19.38). The governors of Macedonia and Bithynia were also proconsuls at this date, whereas the title of the governors of Galatia and Syria was *legatus Augusti pro praetore*. The difference in title reflects differences in their method of appointment and their period in office, but there was no significant difference between the duties and powers of proconsuls and legates (or of governors appointed from the equestrian order by the emperor with the titles *praefectus* or *procurator*, as in Judaea). Governors were commanders-in-chief of any soldiers stationed in their provinces and took command of all major military operations. Such duties hardly affected governors in the provinces visited by Paul (except for the *legatus* of Syria, who commanded four legions). The main civil function of the governor was to act as chief judge in the province. The proconsul of Asia went on tour and held assizes (known as *conventus* in Latin: 19.38) at thirteen major cities in turn (see C. Habicht and G.P. Burton, *Journal of Roman Studies* 65 [1975] pp. 64-106). Precise information about the regular routine of the proconsuls of Macedonia and Achaea is lacking; Gallio was probably conducting assizes at Corinth upon his judicial tribunal (*bema*, 18.12), and Paul's imprisonment at Philippi may indicate that the *duoviri* were expecting a visit from the proconsul of Macedonia, before whom the charges against Paul would be heard (see notes on 16.23).

4) Roman citizens in the provinces. Rome had from the earliest times been far more generous than the cities of classical Greece in granting Roman citizenship to those who were not Romans by birth (see A.5 above). By the middle of the 1st century BC the whole population of the Italian peninsula had been made Roman citizens, and the majority of the population of Rome itself was made up of ex-slaves (or the descendants of ex-slaves) who had received citizenship upon manumission. By about AD 50 there were also a considerable number of Roman citizens resident in the provinces: some were emigrants from Italy or their descendants, whether actual colonists (e.g. at Philippi, 16.21) or unofficial settlers in provincial cities (cf. A.5 above); others might be freed slaves, once owned by Romans, who had returned to their ancestral homes; finally, the emperors had power to confer citizenship on individual foreigners.

A *peregrinus* who was made a Roman changed his nomenclature. In most non-Roman communities a man was known by a personal name (chosen from quite a wide range) and a patronymic. Most male Romans had a set of three names, the characteristic *tria nomina*: the *praenomen*, a personal name, usually one of some dozen common boys' names (including the unimaginative Quintus, 'number 5'; Sextus, 'number 6'; and Decimus, 'number 10'); the *nomen* or *gentilicium*, a 'clan' name often shared by a number of families; and the *cognomen* used to distinguish one particular branch or family among all those with a shared *gentilicium*. A newly-enfranchised citizen often kept his own personal name, or a Latinised version of it, as a *cognomen* and adopted as his own the *praenomen* and *gentilicium* of the Roman to whom he owed his enfranchisement: in the case of a freed slave it would be those of his former owner; in the case of the freeborn, those of the reigning emperor, or of the patron who interceded for them with the emperor. We do not know what *tria nomina* Saul of Tarsus bore as a Roman citizen, but the likelihood is that Paul(l)us was the *cognomen*; it was a Latin word (meaning 'little') which sounded like his personal name, and it had been in use as a *cognomen* among the Roman aristocracy. In that case, unless the ancestor who had been made a Roman citizen (for Paul had been *born* a Roman: 22.28) had also been named Saul, Paul must have dropped his inherited *cognomen*. Since it was Julius Caesar and Augustus who had enfranchised most non-Romans during the appropriate period (*before* Paul's birth), the most likely guess would be 'Gaius Iulius Paul(l)us'.

Although a number of Latin personal or family names appear in *Acts*, only one person (apart from the proconsuls) has a standard *gentilicium* and *cognomen*, Titius Iustus (18.7); and it is not surprising that a prosperous Gentile in the Roman colony at Corinth should himself be a Roman citizen (if he is to be identified with the Gaius who was one of the only two Corinthians who had been baptised by Paul in person [1 Cor. 1.14], he had a convincing set of *tria nomina*, Gaius Titius Iustus). Other men are referred to by single Latin names (e.g. Marcus [12.25, 15.39], Lucius [13.1], Niger [13.1], Aquila [18.2], Crispus [18.8], Scaeva [19.14], Gaius [19.29, 20.4], Secundus [20.4]); since such names were adopted by provincials who were *not* citizens from motives of vanity or ambition, they supply no proof that the persons concerned were Romans (Sherwin-White [1963] p. 157). Paul's companion Silas is included in Paul's assertion of citizen status at Philippi (16.37-8), but it is only from the epistles that we learn that he bore a standard Latin *cognomen*, Silvanus (2 Cor. 1.19, 1 Thess. 1.1, 2 Thess. 1.1, 1 Pet. 5.12). The judicial privileges which Roman citizens could claim are discussed in the notes on 16.37-8.

IV The historicity of *Acts*

In the case of the Homeric poems, M.I. Finley assessed the historicity both of the 'world' of the poems, i.e. the institutions in the background, and of the 'story', i.e. the events narrated in the poems (*The World of Odysseus* 2nd edn, Appendix 1, and *Journal of Hellenic Studies* [1964] 1ff.). An assessment of the historicity of *Acts* may likewise distinguish between the 'world' and the 'story'.

A: *The world of* Acts

Paul's travels in *Acts* are set against a background of urban life in the Hellenised provinces of the Roman empire on either side of the Aegean. The survey in Section III above has supplied the material for concluding that *Acts* gives an accurate picture of that world.

1) Historical geography. It is the accuracy over quite obscure details which is striking. Derbe and Lystra, neither of them well known cities, are correctly situated in the district of Lycaonia (14.6), and Philippi in the first of the four *merides* of Macedonia, if the emendation of 16.12 is accepted. (And, on one controversial interpretation, 16.6 reproduces in Greek a Roman official description for that area, namely Phrygia Galatica: see note on 16.6).

2) Political institutions. Differences in title and status between the chief executives in the cities are registered with precision: politarchs at Thessalonica (17.6); the Clerk of the People at Ephesus (19.35); at Athens the Council of the Areopagus, and not any of the annual magistrates (17.19); and in Philippi, while the *duoviri* are referred to in Greek by the imprecise term *strategoi* (literally = 'generals'), they are attended by lictors (*rhabdouchoi*; literally = 'rod-bearers'), as magistrates in a Roman colony would be, but those of a Greek *polis* would not (16.20, 22, 35-8). The governors of Cyprus, Achaea, and Asia are given the correct title, *anthupatos* (13.7; 18.12; 19.38). Governors are encountered only infrequently, and their characteristic function is the administration of justice (18.12; 19.38).

3) The life of the cities. It was shown above that the sudden gathering of mobs and subsequent demonstrations and even rioting were major problems which greatly concerned the imperial government. The migration of skilled craft workers from city to city (e.g. Lydia [16.15], Aquila and Priscilla [18.2-3], and Paul himself) was also commonplace. Successful and prosperous craftsmen expanded their businesses by buying and training slaves, who then comprised their 'households' (Greek *oikos*, Latin *familia*); such presumably was the *oikos* of Lydia baptised along with her (16.15), and that of the *archisynagogos* Crispus, the whole of which was converted along with him (18.8).

B: *The events of* Acts

Historical criticism of the account of events given in *Acts* can employ any of the three following methods: (i) comparison with other sources; (ii) analyses of the text and its sources which assume that particular elements 'must have' been invented; (iii) *a priori* assumptions that certain kinds of event cannot have occurred, especially those involving the miraculous. The first of these three is obviously the one which is most likely to yield secure results.

For the general historical background to the events in *Acts* there are a few other historical sources, especially Josephus. Comparisons between accounts in *Acts* and in other sources are given in the notes, but it should be noted that where there is a difference, it is by no means obvious that *Acts'* account is the one which should be rejected. The author of *Acts* is a careful and well informed historian, and other historical writers (Josephus in particular) are at least as capable of carelessness, or of distorting the evidence to suit their own purposes, as he is.

In practice, the only other evidence for the activities of Paul is the epistles attributed to him in the New Testament, since there is little else which is directly relevant (an inscription from Delphi does show that L. Junius Gallio was proconsul of Achaea in about 51-2; the evidence for an expulsion of Jews from Rome by Claudius in 49 is hotly debated [see note on 18.1-2]).

The following table reveals a broad concurrence between the list of cities evangelised by Paul according to *Acts* and that of churches to which letters attributed to Paul are addressed.

ACTS		EPISTLES
13.5	Salamis (no report of conversions)	–
13.14-14.24	Pisidian Antioch, Iconium, Lystra, Derbe	*Galatians*
14.25	Perge (no report of conversions)	–
16.12-40	Philippi	*Philippians*

17.1-9	Thessalonica	*1 & 2 Thessalonians*
17.10-14	Beroea (many were converted)	
17.15-34	Athens (two named converts and 'many' others)	
18.1-18	Corinth	*1 & 2 Corinthians*
19	Ephesus	*Ephesians* (authenticity strongly contested)
		Romans (addressed to a church which Paul had not yet visited)
		Colossians (like the church in Laodicea they had not seen Paul in the flesh: Col. 2.1)

For a discussion of apparent discrepancies between *Acts* and the picture Paul himself gives of his activities in his letters, see section II, 3. Though the discrepancies are real, they are not of a kind which would rule out the possibility that the author had access to good and reliable sources, or which would suggest that he was incapable of using them.

The speeches in *Acts* present particular problems. Almost a third of *Acts* consists of speeches, and they contain almost all of the theological content. For that reason, the historicity of the speeches, and of the ideas they contain, is of especial interest to theologians. If it could be shown that the speeches broadly represent what was said on each occasion, or that at least the ideas faithfully represent the teaching of the first Christians, then they would be of the greatest importance in any attempt to reconstruct primitive Christianity.

Theological questions are beyond the scope of this commentary. Speeches, however, are common in all ancient historical works, and are regularly used to fill out, adorn, and elucidate narratives. There is no clear evidence to suggest that the author of *Acts* is using speeches in any way differently from other historical writers. Though shorthand did exist in antiquity, so that it would have been technically possible to transcribe the speeches as they were delivered, there is nothing in the text to suggest that this was done, and the circumstances in which the speeches are delivered seem in most cases to rule out the provision of shorthand writers. In any case, the speeches can at best be no more than summaries of what was said, since in most cases they are far too short to have been delivered in the form in which they are reported.

Some historians use speeches simply as an excuse to demonstrate their rhetorical virtuosity, and in many cases there is no question of their being other than free literary compositions (see for example the speeches Philo puts into the mouth of Moses in his *Life of Moses*). But even the more sober historians would construct speeches for historical characters as they thought appropriate (e.g. Thucydides 1, 22, 1; Polybius 2, 56, 10-11). Tacitus (*Annals* 11, 24) reports a speech of Claudius, the text of which actually survives in an inscription found at Lyon (Dessau no. 212); though Tacitus reports the substance of what was said, his speech is quite different from Claudius' own (and is actually rather better); there are no reports of protests by ancient readers of Tacitus in the Rhône valley that his work was unhistorical. Josephus reports a speech of Herod twice (*War* 1, 373-9 and *Ant.* 15, 127-46); the speeches are quite different. Cassius Dio (38, 36-46) rewrites a speech of Julius Caesar, of which Caesar himself gives his own account in the *Gallic War* (1, 40).

Consequently, in the absence of any positive evidence to the contrary, it is natural to assume that the speeches in *Acts* are the author's own composition, based on what he thought would be plausible, and on what was appropriate for each occasion (compare, for example, Paul's preaching to Jews and 'god-fearers' at Pisidian Antioch at 13.16-41 with his speech to a predominantly Gentile audience in Athens at 17.23-31; or his defence before the Jerusalem mob at 22.1-21, and before Agrippa and Festus at 26.2-23). No doubt he would have incorporated into these speeches any reports he had of what actually was said, and his own conception of the sort of thing that people did say at that stage of the church's history. He gives us, however, no straightforward means by which we can tell what was his own, and what he derived from the reports of others.

The text of letters quoted in direct speech will also have been composed by the author (15.23-7; 23.26-30; see notes on ch. 23).

V The text of *Acts*

Textual problems, where they are relevant to the historical interpretation of *Acts*, are discussed in the notes. One group of texts, however, the so-called 'Western' text, requires special mention.

The best-known manuscript in this group is the Codex Bezae, which was probably written somewhere in Western Europe in the 5th century.

Other attestations to this textual tradition occur predominantly in Latin authors (hence the name 'Western'), but there is some evidence that the tradition existed in the east as well. The 'Western' text of *Acts* contains numerous passages which add to or amplify what is contained in other manuscript traditions. They go well beyond the normal run of glosses and scribal variations. The tradition is a very old one, and can be traced back to the late 2nd century. Suggestions have been put forward that this text is in fact the original text of *Acts*, or that it is a revision by the author himself (or perhaps an early draft). Though these views have not gained general support, it does seem clear that the variations in this text are conscious, rather than mistakes, and the possibility cannot be excluded that they rest on very old traditions.

VI The chronology of *Acts*

Acts refers to several events which can be dated (or at least placed within a broad time span) on the basis of independent evidence (which will be cited at appropriate points in the commentary).

The death of Herod Agrippa I (12.23)	44
Gallio's proconsulship of Achaia (18.12)	51/2
Disturbances in Judaea stirred up by an Egyptian (21.38)	54
Felix replaced as procurator of Judaea (24.27)	59 or 60

The Crucifixion is placed by the Gospels during Pontius Pilate's prefect-ship of Judaea in 26-36, and is most commonly dated by modern scholars to 30 or 33 (J. Finnegan, *Handbook of Biblical Chronology*, pp. 285-301). Paul himself (2 Cor. 11.32) places his visit to Damascus during the reign of Aretas IV of Nabataea, which ended around 40 (Schürer[2] I, p. 581).

This evidence makes it possible to construct the following chronology.

Chs 1-3	(Pentecost and its sequel)	30 or 33
Chs 4-9	(Events down to Paul's conversion)	30 or 33 – before 40
Chs 9-12	(Paul's conversion to James' execution)	late 30s – 44
Chs 13-17	(Paul's first two missionary journeys)	44-9
Ch. 18.1-22	(Paul's stay at Corinth and return to Antioch)	49/50 – 51/2
Chs 19-20	(Paul's third missionary journey)	after 51/2 and before 57/8
Chs 21-4	(Paul's arrest at Jerusalem and hearing before Felix)	57 or 58
Ch. 24.27	(Paul in custody at Caesarea)	57 or 58 – 59 or 60
Chs 25-6	(Paul's appearances before Festus)	59 or 60
Chs 27-8	(Paul's voyage to Rome)	59/60 – 60/1
Ch. 28.30-1	(Paul's two years at Rome)	60-2 or 61-2

Commentary

[*NEB* = *New English Bible*
RSV = *Revised Standard Version*]

Chapter 1

Introduction and dedication; the ascension; the appointment of a twelfth apostle to replace Judas Iscariot.

In the first part of my work, Theophilus, I wrote of all that Jesus did and taught from the beginning... (v. 1) *NEB*; **(In the first book, O Theophilus, I have dealt with all that Jesus began to do and teach...** *RSV*). Like the Gospel of Luke, this book is addressed to one Theophilus (whose identity is undiscoverable), which seems to indicate that they are by the same author. In *Luke* Theophilus is addressed as *kratiste* ('excellent' or 'honourable'), a term of respect applied also to the governors Felix (23.26, 24.2) and Festus (26.25). At this period, titles like this were used very generally, and its use here probably implies no more than that Theophilus was socially superior to the author. Dedications of this kind frequently (but by no means invariably) open ancient works. *Luke* and *Acts* are the only works in the New Testament to open with this sort of conventional dedication, signifying perhaps that the author wishes, by adopting the conventions of Greco-Roman literature, to signal his desire to interpret the Christian message to the Gentile world. *NEB*'s **the first part of my work** begs the question of whether *Luke* and *Acts* are two separate works, or two books of the same work. The word translated 'book' or 'work' is *logos*, a very general term for any account or exposition, which could apply equally either to another work, or another part of the same work (the closest parallel, the introduction to Book 2 of Josephus' *Against Apion*, refers to book 1 as a *biblion*, which is a much more unambiguous way of referring to the previous volume).

Right from the beginning, one of the dominant themes of *Acts* is made prominent. The apostles have been given instructions **through the Holy**

Spirit (v. 2); they are to be **baptised with the Holy Spirit** (v. 5); and they will receive power **when the Holy Spirit comes upon you** (v. 8). Though the word translated Spirit, *pneuma*, is occasionally used in non-Biblical Greek of prophetic inspiration (e.g. Strabo 9, 419), its more normal meaning is breath or wind, and the usage here certainly has its origins in the Greek of the Septuagint translation of the Jewish scriptures, where it is used for the Hebrew word *ruah*. This word too can mean wind (e.g. Jon. 1.4) or breath (Lam. 4.20), but it is especially used of the spirit of God, active in creation (e.g. Gen. 1.2) or in inspiration (e.g. Num. 11.25). Prophetic visions and utterances are said to occur 'in the Spirit' (*en pneumati*) (e.g. Ezek. 37.1), a usage which is found also in writers in the New Testament (e.g. Rev. 1.10) and in the early church (*Didache* 11, 7-9). In *Acts*, the Spirit is used as a mark of God's approval, and later the gift of the Spirit is the guarantee that such controversial acts as the admission of non-Jews to the church are in accordance with God's plan.

The brief account of Jesus' post-resurrection appearances neither summarises the ending of *Luke*, nor fits very easily as a continuation of the narrative. Some degree of clumsiness in expression here suggests the possibility of later modifications to the text, either to make *Luke* and *Acts* free-standing when the two books were separated, or to smooth out supposed inconsistencies between the two accounts.

The eleven remaining apostles gather to elect a twelfth as a substitute for Judas Iscariot. The list given is identical to that of *Luke* 6.14-16. The name of **Simon the Zealot** (v. 13) has aroused speculation because the Zealots, according to Josephus (*War* 4, 160-1), were one of the more extreme factions involved in the revolt against Rome in 66. There is, however, no reason to believe that the term was applied to militant nationalists before that date, and in fact the term can be used simply to express outstanding piety; Paul (*Acts* 22.3) is made to describe himself in his youth as a zealot for God (*NEB*: **ardent in God's service**). Simon's name cannot be used as evidence for a connection between the early Christian movement and radical revolutionaries. Before the new apostle is selected, Peter gives what amounts to the author's definition of an apostle: **One of those who bore us company all the while we had the Lord Jesus with us, coming and going, from John's ministry of baptism until the day when he was taken from us** (vv. 21-2). This is consistent with the normal treatment of the apostles in *Acts* as a closed group of twelve, which is why Paul, despite his claims in his Letters, is not regarded as an apostle (apart from a curious anomaly at 14.4 and 14.14). In the rest of *Acts*, the only one of the apostles who plays a significant part is Peter, with John and James in supporting roles.

Chapter 2

The gift of the Spirit at Pentecost; Peter's first speech; the growth of the community.

At the feast of **Pentecost** (celebrated seven weeks after the Passover) the new community makes its first public appearance. As a narrative, this episode is somewhat disjointed. The Spirit comes upon the gathered Christians inside a house, and then suddenly they seem to be out of doors, addressing an audience consisting of **devout Jews drawn from every nation under heaven** (v. 5), who were **living in Jerusalem** (v. 5) (that is to say, they were permanent residents rather than visitors). If by 'every nation under heaven' the author means the civilised world as he knew it, then he is not exaggerating the extent of the Jewish diaspora. The geographer Strabo (early 1st century; quoted by Josephus, *Ant.* 14, 115) asserted that 'this nation (the Jews) has already made its way into every city, and it is not easy to find a place in the inhabited world which has not admitted these people'. Jewish communities are known to have existed in cities from western Iran to Spain (see Schürer[2] III [1] pp. 3-85). Although the list of peoples and regions given in vv. 9-11 gives a fairly accurate picture of the geographical spread of Jewish settlement, it does have some odd features. **Parthians** are presumably inhabitants of the Parthian empire, (Rome's neighbour to the east and the other 'great power' of the day) rather than actual Parthians, in the sense of members of the Iranian tribe which invaded the Seleucid kingdom in the middle of the 3rd century BC. **Medes, Elamites** and **inhabitants of Mesopotamia** would also fall within the lands ruled by the Parthians, and are no doubt included to reinforce the impression of geographical spread, and for exotic colour (and presumably in the case of the Medes and the Elamites, also because of their biblical associations). The inhabitants of **Judaea** come rather strangely at this point; they would presumably be locals, and there is no mystery about their understanding what is being said; though no doubt Galileans spoke with a marked accent (see perhaps *Luke* 22.59) there is no suggestion elsewhere in the New Testament that Jesus or his disciples had difficulty in making themselves understood in Jerusalem; the 'ironing out' of a local accent would be a rather feeble miracle. The names **Cappadocia, Pontus, Asia, Phrygia,** and **Pamphylia** cover much (but not all) of Asia Minor. **Egypt and the districts of Libya around Cyrene** both had well-established Jewish communities. The next group mentioned are probably better referred to as **Roman visitors** rather than the 'visitors from Rome' of *NEB* and *RSV*, because the Greek *Rhomaioi* surely means 'citizens of the

Roman state' rather than 'persons originating from the town of Rome'. It would be tempting to take **both Jews and proselytes** as a description of these Roman citizens (i.e. some had been born Jews, and others had been converted), were it not for the fact that what follows, **Cretans and Arabs**, is clearly parallel to it. Various attempts have been made to explain the oddities of this list on the basis of its being a modification of a document produced for other purposes (e.g. a list of lands claimed by the Roman empire, or a catalogue of mission fields, or an enumeration of the regions of the world from an astrological treatise). None has won widespread support. Attempts were made to remove **Judaea** by emendation even in antiquity: Tertullian (*Adv. Iud.* 7, 4) and Augustine (*contra Epistulam Fundamenti* 10) have Armenia instead; Jerome, commenting on Isa 11.11ff., has Syria.

The number of languages involved need not have been very great. Greek or Aramaic would be the native language of most, if not all, present. Some may have spoken Persian or Arabic. Native vernaculars were spoken in the countryside in several regions (e.g. Eastern Anatolia and Egypt), but it is unlikely that many Jews, who settled mainly in towns, would speak any of these as a native language (and it is clear from v. 8 that it is each person's **native language** which he is hearing, not some other language he might have learnt). It is possible that those identified as Roman citizens spoke Latin, but by the middle of the 1st century there were already many 'Roman citizens' whose first language was Greek and who had no real knowledge of Latin. When the emperor Claudius discovered that a leading man from a Greek province, who was a Roman citizen, could not understand Latin, he stripped him of his citizenship (Suetonius *Claudius* 16, 2). That most Diaspora Jews could understand only the language of the particular area in which they were resident is shown by the production of the first written translation of the Hebrew scriptures in the 3rd and 2nd centuries BC, the *Septuagint*. This Greek version was probably made in the first instance to meet the needs of the Jews of Alexandria. It is a striking fact that it is still disputed among scholars whether the most learned of Alexandrian Jews, Philo, was able to read the Hebrew originals of the biblical texts on which he commented. In the same way, to meet the needs of Jews in the east, from the 1st century AD onwards *Targums*, Aramaic translations of the books of the bible, were produced (though many are paraphrases rather than translations, and some contain an element of commentary; see Schürer[2] I, pp. 99-105).

It is tempting to compare this episode with the 'speaking in tongues' discussed by Paul in 1 Cor. 14, but they are clearly quite distinct phenomena. In *Acts* what is remarkable is that everyone understands what is being said; when people 'spoke in tongues' in Corinth, nobody understood what was being said.

RSV's translation **They are filled with new wine** (v. 13) is much closer to the Greek than *NEB*'s **They have been drinking**. There is no new wine at Pentecost, so presumably the phrase is a proverbial allusion to widespread drunkenness when the year's new wine first becomes drinkable. Here it simply gives a lead to the joke with which Peter begins his speech.

At this stage in *Acts* the author's source seems to be a series of disconnected anecdotes and reports of incidents which do not form a coherent narrative. He joins them together with link passages of which vv. 42-7 is an example. These passages in general simply record the growth of the community, and the general harmony and goodness which prevailed. The mention of **breaking bread** (v. 46), whether it refers to a proto-eucharist or some other communal meal, is unexplained, and so would mean little to a non-Christian.

Chapter 3

Peter and John heal a cripple at the gate of the temple; Peter preaches in the Portico of Solomon.

In the first section of *Acts* the followers of Jesus are represented as being assiduous in their worship at the temple, and so within the mainstream of orthodox Judaism. The temple had originally been founded by King Solomon, and had been rebuilt in a magnificent style by Herod I between 20 and 12 BC. For orthodox Jews it was the only place where sacrificial offerings to the God of Israel could lawfully be made, and the most important point of conflict between Jews and Samaritans was the latter's insistence on maintaining the status of their own sanctuary on Mt Gerizim. It is undoubtedly significant that the first miraculous healing performed by the new church takes place at the heart of Judaism; the break between Christians and Jews, the author seems to be suggesting, was not initiated by the Christians. **The gate of the temple called 'Beautiful Gate'** (v. 2) cannot be identified. No other source describes any of the gates into the outer enclosure around the temple (the Court of the Gentiles) or into the inner enclosure (where only Jews could enter) as 'beautiful'. There is no way of deciding where this incident may have taken place (for an exhaustive discussion of the possibilities see BC V, pp. 479-86).

On entering the temple, they go to **Solomon's Portico** (v. 11), a stoa or colonnade, which later became a regular meeting place for the Christians (5.13), and in which Jesus is known to have walked (*John* 10.23). Josephus (*War* 5, 185) mentions a colonnade in Solomon's original temple on the eastern side, but its relationship with the one mentioned here is unclear. Like the 'Beautiful Gate', 'Solomon's Portico' cannot be identified.

Clearly it was a place where groups of people could meet (which was one of the functions of a stoa), and Peter briefly addresses the crowd there.

Chapter 4

Peter and John are arrested and examined by the High Priest and his associates; they are cautioned and released.

By preaching within the temple, Peter and John attract the attention of the authorities. This is the beginning of a series of persecutions of the church. The author presents it as, first of all, a gratuitous and unprovoked attack, and, second, as the action of a small but powerful faction among the Jews.

They are first approached by the **priests** (v. 1), who had the exclusive right to perform sacrifices at the temple. The office passed by inheritance in the male line in families who traced their ancestry to Aaron, the brother of Moses. A small minority of these families, from whose ranks the High Priests were drawn, were very wealthy, but the majority were not well off. The hereditary priests were so numerous that they were grouped into 24 'courses', each of which took part in the temple rituals in turn, for a week at a time. With them was **the Controller of the Temple** (v. 1) (cf. *Luke* 22.52). The Greek word used, *strategos* ('general'), is also used by Josephus of an office held by two named individuals. Rabbinical sources refer to two posts: the *sagan* who was in overall charge of order in the temple; and subordinate officers of the *sagan*. It is unclear which is being referred to here (BC IV, p. 40).

The Sadducees (v. 1), however, are not officers at all, but members of a religious 'party'. At 5.17 they are referred to as a *hairesis* ('sect' or 'party'). They are several times mentioned together with their great rivals the Pharisees. Josephus (*War* 2, 162-6; *Ant.* 13, 171-3; 18, 11-17) applies the term *hairesis* to three groups (the third being the Essenes) who were adherents of three forms of philosophy. According to his account, the main distinguishing feature is the view of each about free will and predestination: the Essenes believe all events are predestined; the Sadducees maintain the complete freedom of the will; the Pharisees hold that some events are determined, while others are not. It is likely that Josephus is attempting to represent the Jewish religious 'parties' as philosophical schools; the question of free will was hotly contested among contemporary Greek philosophers, and one of the meanings of *hairesis* is 'philosophical school'. Rabbinical sources refer in Hebrew to *zadduqim* who were the opponents (before the Roman capture of Jerusalem in AD 70) of the 'Sages' (*hakamim*) whom the rabbis regarded as their own predecessors. The points at issue were in the main detailed matters of Temple ritual and law. The

Sadducees regarded only the *Torah* (the first five books of the Bible) as authoritative, whereas the Pharisees gave weight also to the body of traditional exegesis. At any rate, the Sadducees are clearly adherents of a religious 'party', not holders of offices. The author of *Acts* evidently believed that the majority of Temple priests would be Sadducees (cf. 5.17); for Josephus also they were drawn from the ruling aristocracy, which at Jerusalem meant some of the priestly families (*Ant.* 13, 298; 18, 17). One explanation of the name connects it with Zadok, High Priest in the reign of King David; only his descendants were supposed to hold the office of High Priest.

The reason alleged for their arrest is the authorities' objection to their **proclaiming the resurrection from the dead** (v. 2). The Sadducees rejected the resurrection of the dead (for which there is no authority in the *Torah*); this was one of the principal issues which divided them from the Pharisees. Josephus confirms that the doctrine of the Sadducees makes the soul die with the body (*Ant.* 18, 16; *War* 2, 165: 'they reject the survival of the soul and penalties and rewards in Hades'). The author represents the apostles as innocent victims caught in a quarrel between the two religious 'parties'.

They are brought before a body consisting of **the Jewish rulers, elders, and doctors of the law** (v. 5). The first two terms are imprecise descriptions of members of the governing council at Jerusalem called the Sanhedrin, of which this is represented as being a meeting. The 'doctors of the law', on the other hand, were a distinct quasi-professional group in 1st century Judaea. The Greek words *grammateis* ('scribes'), *nomikoi* ('lawyers'), and *nomodidaskaloi* ('teachers of the law') are used in the New Testament to refer to the group who were described in Hebrew as *soferim*; Josephus refers to them as 'sophists', 'sacred scribes', or 'interpreters of the sacred laws'. It was not birth, as in the case of priests, but learning which qualified a Jew to be a scribe. This learning was acquired by 'sitting at the feet' of an acknowledged scribe of an earlier generation. Their function, apart from teaching, was the interpretation and application of Jewish law embodied in the *Torah*, the 'Books of Moses' (the first five books of the Bible). On the basis of this 'written law' successive generations of scribes built up an elaborate body of 'oral law', handed down by word of mouth from generation to generation until it was codified in the *Mishnah* at the end of the 2nd century. The scribes enjoyed much greater prestige among ordinary Jews than did the aristocracy drawn from some of the priestly families (see Goodman, *The Ruling Class of Judaea*, pp. 73-4, 123-4; Schürer[2] II, pp. 322-36).

Specifically mentioned as members of the council are **Annas the High Priest, Caiaphas, Jonathan, Alexander, and all who were of the high-priestly family** (v. 6). There was at any one time a single High Priest at the head of the Temple cult in Jerusalem. On ceremonial occasions he wore special vestments and he alone could enter the innermost room in the Temple, the Holy of Holies, and that on only one day in the year, the Day of Atonement. The office had been one usually held for life until Herod was made king by the Romans in 40 BC. Since Herod, unlike his predecessors of the Hasmonean dynasty since 152 BC, was not of priestly descent and could not combine the position of secular ruler with the High Priesthood, he sought to curtail the prestige of the office by appointing and dismissing High Priests at his pleasure (and by keeping the ceremonial vestments under his own control between the great festivals). These practices continued after Judaea had been turned into a province under a Roman governor in AD 6. For Josephus this event marked the restoration of 'aristocracy' in Judaea, with the High Priest exercising the *prostasia* of the Jewish nation; this *prostasia* was the function of acting as the representative (*prostates*) of the nation before the alien overlords. Nevertheless, lacking life tenure, and being the appointees of the Gentile rulers (until AD 41; from 41 to 66 of the descendants of Herod), the High Priests exercised relatively little power as individuals.

Annas represents the Hebrew name *Hanan*, and the same man is referred to by Josephus as *Ananus* (son of Seth), and according to him this man was appointed high priest in AD 6, but replaced in AD 15 (*Ant.* 18, 26, 34), while the office was held from AD 18 to 36 by Joseph Caiaphas, described at *John* 18.13 as Annas' son-in-law. At *Luke* 3.1-2 it appears to be stated that Annas and Caiaphas held the office jointly in AD 29. There is evidently some confusion about the succession of High Priests, and Josephus' record should be preferred; at this date, during Pilate's governorship, Caiaphas, not Annas, was *the* High Priest in office.

In the phrase translated both by *NEB* and by *RSV* 'all who were of the high-priestly family' the 'the' represents nothing in the Greek. A more accurate rendering would be 'of high-priestly stock'. In the period from Herod to the rebellion against Rome in AD 66 the High Priesthood was the preserve, not of a single family, but of a circle of three or four families. Josephus describes one of Herod's appointees as being of 'high-priestly *genos*' (*Ant.* 15, 40), using the very same phrase. It may be that it was to members of these families that the Mishnah alluded as 'sons of the High Priests' (see Schürer[2] II, pp. 233-6).

This episode is rounded off with another 'link passage', recording the continuing success of the community, and their high reputation. We are briefly introduced to **Joseph, surnamed by the apostles Barnabas (which means 'Son of Exhortation'), a Levite, by birth a Cypriot** (v. 36). Later Barnabas is found bringing the newly converted Saul to the apostles in Jerusalem (9.27), and he is active in Antioch (11.22; 11.25; 11.30; 12.25; 13.1). Levites were supposedly descended from one of the twelve Patriarchs, Levi son of Jacob. The priests formed one branch of the descendants of Levi, the house of Aaron. All other descendants of Levi served as musicians, guards, doorkeepers etc. in the Temple, but were excluded from the 'Court of Priests' and the sacrifices. It is not obvious what Hebrew original with the meaning 'Son of Exhortation' may lie behind the name Barnabas. Although we have already been told (2.44-5) that among Christians everything was held in common (v. 32), this is the only incident of the contribution of private property to a common pool of which we are told.

Chapter 5

Ananias and Sapphira are struck dead for holding back some of their property; the apostles are arrested, freed by an angel, and brought to trial on the next day; they are defended by Gamaliel, and released with a flogging and a warning.

The episode of Ananias and Sapphira is put here presumably as a contrast to the generosity of Barnabas. It seems to have no context within the general narrative, and is probably an example of a detached story which the author has found and fitted in where it seems appropriate. There is no point in speculating what may lie behind this strange episode.

The new community is now referred to for the first time as the **church** (v. 11). The Greek word translated 'church' is *ekklesia*, which normally means the assembly of the citizens of a *polis*, a city (and it is used in this sense of the assembly of Ephesus at 19.32, 39-40). In the Septuagint, however, it is used as the translation of the Hebrew word *qahal* (or, occasionally, related words). Sometimes (e.g. Deut 9.10) it seems to have a purely political sense (and *Hebrews* 12.23 may use it in a similar sense). Usually, however, especially in the phrase *ekklesia kyriou*, 'the assembly of the Lord' (e.g. Deut 23.2), or *ekklesia theou*, 'the assembly of God', it seems to mean the people of God (and this is why the word is translated 'when they were assembled' in Stephen's summary of Jewish history at 7.38). The use of this term by Christians is a consequence of their claim to be the new Israel, the legitimate heirs to God's promises. *Acts* normally uses *ekklesia* to mean the individual Christian community (e.g. 8.1; 13.1; 15.3; 18.22). Where it is a question of a number of communities, the plural is used (e.g. 14.23; 15.41; 16.5). (For possible exceptions, see the notes on 9.31 and 20.28).

The next day, following their arrest, the apostles are brought to trial before the 'Sanhedrin', that is the full senate of the Israelite nation (v. 21). *Sanhedrin*, a Hebrew loan word from Greek, represents the Greek word *synedrion*, and 'senate' represents the Greek word *gerousia*, 'a body of old men'. Both words refer to a single institution, the ruling Council and Supreme Court of Judaea under the overall authority of the Roman governors (Sanhedrin is one of the terms used in the Mishnah for the supreme court at Jerusalem before AD 70). About the composition and powers of this body there is great controversy because of the discrepancies between the New Testament and Josephus on the one hand, and the Rabbinical sources on the other. For example, the former always show the ruling council at Jerusalem being presided over by the High Priest (as in this case), but the latter identify the successive heads of the two schools of Pharisaic thought as presidents and vice-presidents of the Sanhedrin. Attempts to reconcile the two accounts have included suggestions that the High Priest presided over 'political' sessions, the leaders of the 'sages' over 'judicial' ones (S. Safrai in S. Safrai and M. Stern [eds], *The Jewish People in the 1st Century* I, pp. 388-9); or that there were three distinct 'councils' in Jerusalem: a 'political' Sanhedrin'; a 'religious' court; and a municipal council (e.g. E.M. Smallwood, *The Jews under Roman Rule*, pp. 32f.; see Schürer[2] II, pp. 199-226; Goodman, *The Ruling Class of Judaea*, pp. 112-6).

When the apostles refuse to stop their teaching, they are defended by **a Pharisee called Gamaliel, a teacher of the law held in high regard by all the people** (v. 34). For the Pharisees as a religious 'party' at variance with the Sadducees, see the note on 4.1. While the Gospels, which usually link them with the 'scribes' (see note on 4.5), depict them as self-righteous and nit-picking legalists, Josephus gives a favourable picture, but one which also stresses their strict religious observance and precision in interpreting the laws (*War* 1, 110; 2, 162, 166; *Ant.* 18, 12-15). Josephus also claims that he was a Pharisee himself (*Life* 12). As with the organisation of the Sanhedrin, there are difficulties over reconciling this evidence with the rabbinical sources, in which the main opponents of the *zadduqim* are described as *hakamim* ('sages'; cf. 4.5). The latter were regarded by the rabbis as admirable and their own predecessors. But the rabbinical sources also criticise a group they describe as *perushim* (possibly = 'separatists') for much the same faults as those attributed to the Pharisees in the Gospels, and in one place in the Mishnah we find the *zadduqim* reproving the *perushim*. Gamaliel is presumably one of the scribes, and is perhaps the Gamaliel mentioned in Josephus as the father of the Pharisee Simon, an opponent of Josephus in 66-7 (*Life* 190ff.; *War* 4, 159). The rabbinical sources speak in the highest terms of Gamaliel I, the grandfather of Gamaliel II who taught at Jamnia ca. AD 90; Gamaliel I was head of the Pharisaic school founded by Hillel, from whom he was descended. At 22.3 Paul is made to claim that he has been a pupil of Gamaliel (see Schürer[2] II, pp. 388-403; Goodman, *The Ruling Class of Judaea*, pp. 82-4; J. Bowker, *Jesus and the Pharisees*).

Gamaliel's case is that they are better left alone, because if God is with them, they cannot be defeated, while if he is not, their movement will collapse of its own accord. He gives two examples of failed revolts. **Theudas** (v. 36) may be the same man as the Theudas referred to by Josephus (*Ant.* 20, 97-9) who was executed by the governor Cuspius Fadus (ca. 44-6) after convincing a large number of the common people to follow him to the Jordan. This event took place several years after this point in the narrative of *Acts*, and forty years *after* the revolt led by Judas the Galilean, who is described in the next verse as coming *after* Theudas. It can be no more than a coincidence that Josephus goes on to describe the execution of the *sons* of Judas (*Ant.* 20, 102); it is an extremely unconvincing hypothesis that the author of *Acts* had read, and misunderstood, a work which Josephus did not publish until AD 93-4. The author must have furnished from his own memory two illustrations of self-proclaimed prophets to support the argument put into Gamaliel's mouth and his memory must have been very unreliable in matters of chronology (cf. the account of the census of Quirinus in *Luke* 2.1-5). The second example is **Judas the Galilean at the time of the census** (v. 37). At the beginning of the Gospel of Luke, the nativity of Jesus is dated by reference to the 'first census' conducted when Quirinus was governor of Syria (*Luke* 2.2). Josephus reports that when Augustus decided in AD 6 to depose and exile Archelaus, who had ruled Judaea as ethnarch since the death of his father Herod I, and to turn Judaea into a province, he ordered Quirinus, the governor of Syria (P. Sulpicius Quirinus, consul in 12 BC), to conduct a census of property in Judaea (*Ant.* 17, 355; 18, 1-2, 26). (For the insoluble problems presented by the indications of chronology in *Luke* 1-2, see Schürer[2] I, pp. 400-27). Josephus also reports that resistance to the census was incited by one Judas, and he describes a rebellion far more serious than is implied in Gamaliel's words (*War* 2, 118; *Ant.* 18, 4-9). At one point Josephus describes this Judas as a man from Gamala in Gaulanitis (modern Golan; *Ant.* 18, 4), but elsewhere, like the author of *Acts*, he calls him a Galilean (*War* 2, 118; *Ant.* 18, 23; 20, 102).

Chapter 6

A dispute within the church leads the apostles to appoint a group of seven Hellenised Christians to help them; one of them, Stephen, is brought before the Council on a charge of blasphemy.

The events narrated in ch. 6 are something of a watershed in *Acts*. Unfortunately, it is more than usually difficult to work out exactly what is going on. We are told that a dispute broke between what *NEB* describes as **those** of them who spoke Greek and those who spoke the language of the Jews (v. 1), a phrase more accurately rendered by *RSV* as the Hellenists murmured against the Hebrews. These groups appear in *Acts* here for the first time, and it is not at all clear who they are. A *Hellenistes* (not a common Greek word) should mean someone who has been Hellenised, that is, one who has absorbed Greek culture. It is natural to assume that these are Jews of the Diaspora who are Greek speaking and live in a Greek environment. We know that many Diaspora Jews were primarily Greek speaking (see notes on 2.9-11), and Diaspora communities showed considerable familiarity with other elements of Greek culture; for example, the Alexandrian Jew Philo found it worthwhile to write substantial commentaries (in Greek) on the books of the Hebrew bible, explaining them in terms derived from contemporary Greek philosophy. Presumably, then, this group consists of Diaspora Jews living in Jerusalem. In that case, the Hebrews would be Jews from Palestine and the east, whose language would be Aramaic. There does seem to have been a marked linguistic division in Jerusalem. Later in *Acts* (21.40; 22.2) Paul is able to calm down the crowd by addressing them in Aramaic (or possibly Hebrew); the tribune who has arrested him (21.37) is surprised when he speaks to him in Greek. Clearly, however, the issue here is not purely linguistic. The Hellenists complained that their widows were being overlooked in the daily distribution (v. 1). There is nothing surprising about any group of Jews giving alms in a systematic way to widows and other needy people, though it is not obvious how this can be reconciled with the report at 2.44-5 that all property was held in common. The apostles respond by appointing a group of seven (presumably) Hellenists to deal with these matters (v. 3), that is to say, to wait at table (v. 2), while the apostles devote themselves to prayer and the ministry of the Word (vv. 3-4). It may be significant that all of the seven have Greek names (but so do two of the twelve apostles: Andrew and Philip). One of them, Nicolaus, is identified as a convert from Antioch, from which we can safely infer that the rest were all born Jews. The apostles (and the 'Hebrews' generally) now slip into the background, and the rest of *Acts* is, with a few exceptions, about the Hellenised Jews of the Diaspora, and Gentile converts. Despite their appointment to wait at table, the only two of the seven of whom we are told anything more, Stephen and Philip, immediately become involved in public preaching, which leads to a reaction going far beyond the minor harassment which they have experienced up to now, and culminates in the killing of one of the seven, Stephen, the first Christian martyr. It is interesting, and possibly significant, that the agitation against Stephen is stirred up by a group which itself is a part of the Jewish Diaspora, the Synagogue of Freedmen, comprising Cyrenians and Alexandrians and people from Cilicia and Asia (v. 9). The Greek word translated as 'freedmen' is a loan-word from Latin. The Latin term *libertinus* (plural *libertini*) applies only to Roman citizens, who were divided into two categories, the freeborn (*ingenui*), and those who had once been slaves and had been formally freed by their Roman owner (*libertini*). Jews by birth who had become slaves owned and freed by Romans, or Gentile slaves (or freedmen) of Roman citizens converted to Judaism, would count as 'freedmen'. But whether enough such persons would have migrated to Jerusalem after being freed (probably in Italy) to form a sizeable group is uncertain, so a very ancient correction to the text, *Libustinon* (Libyans) instead of *Libertinon* (freedmen), is very attractive. It would supply a fifth geographical term, and Libyans would be the geographic neighbours of Cyrenians. It is in any case unclear from the text whether we are dealing with one group, or five, or some number between one and five. The word 'comprising' in the *NEB* translation represents nothing in the Greek, and is presumably inserted because the translators favoured the view that only one group is involved; but other interpretations are perfectly possible. The impression that what is going on here is a quarrel among Hellenised Diaspora Jews is to some extent contradicted by the report that Stephen's teaching attracted, among others, **very many of the priests** (v. 7), who would surely be local people, classified as 'Hebrews' (see note on 4.1). The stress on their adherence is an indication of a traditional Jewish respect for the hereditary priesthood. The author is reassuring us that Stephen's preaching, which provoked the first martyrdom, was of a kind which proved acceptable even to the most traditional groups.

Chapter 7

Stephen addresses the Council; he is killed by stoning.

Stephen's response to the accusation of blasphemy (but note that the Greek *blasphemia* has a wider meaning than 'blasphemy'; 'slander' or 'abuse' is closer) is a long speech summarising the history of the Jews from Abraham to Moses, derived largely from *Genesis* and *Exodus*, whose theme is that the Jews have always rejected those sent to them by God. It includes disparaging remarks about the temple (vv. 44-50), which tends to give credence to the accusations made against him: **'This man is for ever saying things against this holy place...'** (6.13), and may explain why in the earlier section of *Acts* the author is so insistent on the devotion of the apostles to worship in the temple. Diaspora Jews had, of necessity, developed forms of worship, based on the synagogue, which were independent of the Temple; it is not surprising that the status of the Temple would arouse strong feelings among them.

Stephen's uncompromising reply provokes an uproar, in the course of which **they made one rush at him and, flinging him out of the city, set about stoning him** (v. 58). It is not clear whether the author is trying to describe a judicial execution or a lynching. It is highly probable that Jewish courts could not have death sentences carried out without the permission of the Roman governor (though this claim has been strongly contested: see the arguments in Sherwin-White [1963] pp. 36-47, Schürer² II, pp. 219-23, and D.R. Stackpole in E. Bammel [ed.], *The Trial of Jesus*, pp. 59-63). It appears to be directly asserted in *John* 18.31 ('The Jews answered: "We are not allowed to put any man to death" '), and it is implied in the narratives of Jesus' trial in *Matthew* and *Mark*. But it is not clear from *Luke* (23.1-25) whether or not the author believed that the Sanhedrin could have death sentences carried out officially. Another difficulty arises from the implication in v. 60 that Stephen met his death by being pelted with stones: **he fell on his knees...** (which is how the martyrdom is depicted in later Christian art). According to the Mishnah, execution by stoning involved the condemned man being thrown from a height and, if he survived, having a single stone dropped onto him; only if he survived that was there a mass stoning (*mSanhedrin* 6:1-4). How far sentences had actually been carried out according to these rules in Jerusalem before AD 70, and whether the author would be aware that this is what an official stoning involved, is uncertain. So it is impossible to decide whether the author had been informed that Stephen was put to death under a formal sentence of the Sanhedrin.

We are told, almost in passing, of the entry on to the scene of Paul, who will dominate the later chapters of *Acts*: **The witnesses laid their coats at the feet of a young man named Saul** (v. 58). (For Paul/Saul's names see note on 13.9). It was the duty of the witnesses to participate in a stoning.

Chapter 8

Persecution drives the Christians from Jerusalem; Philip converts Samaritans and an Ethiopian eunuch.

The legal status of the **violent persecution for the church in Jerusalem** (v. 1) is unclear, and perhaps deliberately left so. The author has insisted that the Christian community was held in high regard by the people (e.g. 2.47, 4.34), which would not fit well with reports of mob violence against them. Besides, he seems to be less well-informed on the details of life in Jerusalem than he shows himself to be later about the cities of Asia Minor and Greece, so it is not clear that he would be aware of what did or did not constitute 'official' rather than 'unofficial' action. It is, however, clear from Josephus' narrative that the 'rule of law' in the modern sense hardly prevailed at Jerusalem in these years. In these circumstances it is perfectly possible both that there were popular riots against the Christians and that the authorities were afraid to use force against them **for fear of being stoned by the people** (5.26). The report that **Stephen was given burial** (v. 2) is a further indication that his stoning was a lynching, not a judicial execution, because according to the rules in the Mishnah burial should not be permitted for a victim of an 'official' stoning. Saul/Paul is represented as being especially active in this persecution, and to have arrested and imprisoned a number of people. We are not told by what authority or in what capacity he acted; the author is simply concerned to establish him as a prominent persecutor, in preparation for the story of his conversion.

The whole community is scattered through Judaea and Samaria, **except the apostles** (v. 1). It may be that the apostles had a greater sense of their responsibilities than the others, though it would be odd if they, the most prominent members of the movement, who had been active in preaching, and some of whom had been arrested and flogged, could hope to remain untouched by the persecution. This may be an indication that what is going on is indeed an argument among Diaspora Jews, and that the apostles, as 'Hebrews', were regarded as being safely within the mainstream of 'orthodox' Judaism, and so relatively immune.

The scattering of the Jerusalem Christians is the occasion of the spread of the message beyond the 'orthodox' Jews of Palestine. A group of Samaritans and an Ethiopian eunuch are converted, and in both cases the agent is Philip, one of the seven 'Hellenists'. This marks a first step in the expansion of the Christians which will ultimately lead to the admission of Gentile converts, but that crucial step is not yet unambiguously taken.

Philip travels first to **a city in Samaria** (v. 5). The reading 'city', without the definite article, is less well attested in the manuscript tradition than the alternative '*the* city of Samaria', but this grammatical construction, although natural in English, is very awkward in Greek; and if '*the* city' were taken to be the town called Samaria in the Old Testament, that town had been renamed Sebaste by Herod and was a pagan *polis*, a very odd place for Philip to begin his evangelising in the country of the Samaritans (and we hear later [v. 9] that Simon, whom Philip baptises here, had practised magic in *the* city, and amazed the nation [*ethnos*] of Samaria, which must mean the Samaritans). Which was this city then? That Simon Magus was born at Gitta in Samaria according to Justin Martyr (*Apol.* I 26: Justin calls Gitta a 'village', *kome*) is not much help. Surely a major centre is indicated, and that is most likely to have been Shechem, near the Samaritans' holy place on Mt Gerizim (refounded by Vespasian as Neapolis, whence Nablus, the home of the surviving Samaritans).

A number of Samaritans **were baptised** (v. 12). Baptism (a purificatory immersion in water) was at this period a normal (and indeed obligatory) part of the ritual for admitting Gentile converts to Judaism (Schürer[2] III [1] pp. 173-4). The immediate precedent for Christian baptism, however, must have been the baptism of John the Baptist, which was intended for Jews, and signified repentance, not admission to a new community (Matt. 3.7, Mark 1.4-5, Luke 3.3). Nevertheless, Gentile converts later, if they were familiar with Jewish practice, would not have been surprised at being required to undergo baptism before becoming Christians. The method of baptism is not specified. John baptised in the river Jordan. Where no river was convenient some other method must have been used. The *Didache* tells us the preferred methods early in the history of the church: 'baptise... in running water; if you have no running water, baptise in other water; if you cannot baptise in cold water, baptise in warm water; if you have neither, pour water three times on the head' (7, 1-3).

The origin of the Samaritans is obscure. Their separation from the other Jews may have taken place as early as the 4th century BC. Their relationship with other Jews was marked by hostility, especially after the destruction of their temple on Mt Gerizim by the Hasmonean rulers of Judaea between 111 and 107 BC (Schürer[2] I, p. 210 n. 22). Like other Jews they regarded the *Torah* as authoritative, and like the Sadducees (but not the Pharisees) they did not accept the authority of any writings or rulings not found in the *Torah*. Their principal difference from other Jews was their maintenance of a temple on Mt Gerizim rather than at Jerusalem. Consequently they are regarded as inadequate Jews rather than as Gentiles. They could be admitted to the Christian community without raising all the issues which the admission of Gentiles involved. Nevertheless their admission is referred for confirmation to the apostles, and God's approval is guaranteed when **they received the Holy Spirit** (v. 17).

The encounter with Simon is both intriguing and puzzling. He is said to have won over the Samaritans by his practice of *magia* (translated here as 'magic': v. 11). In other words, he is a *magos*. A.D. Nock, in his paper on 'Paul and the Magus' (BC V, pp. 164-88; reprinted in his *Essays on Religion in the Ancient World* I, 308-30) traced the process by which the name of a member of a priestly caste among the Iranians (similar to the Brahmins of India) came to mean a 'wonder worker', a professional 'vendor of curses and philtres'. Both Arnuphis, the Egyptian companion of Marcus Aurelius (Dio Cassius 72, 8, 4) and Apollonius of Tyana, whom Caracalla honoured as a hero long after his death (Dio Cassius 78, 18, 4), are described as *magoi* (although it is interesting that Apollonius' biographer indignantly rejects the word: Philostratus, *Life of Apollonius* 1, 2). Dio's contempt for Apollonius does not prevent him from believing that while he was in Ephesus he miraculously learned of the death of Domitian in Rome (Dio Cassius 67, 18, 1). We meet another *magos* in *Acts* at 13.6.

The *magoi* of *Matthew* 2.1-12 seem to be astrologers.

There may, however, be more to Simon than this. The Samaritans said of him: 'This man...is that power of God which is called "The Great Power" ' (v. 10), an odd phrase which seems to suggest someone making claims to religious authority, rather than a local wonder-worker. In the next century Celsus, in an anti-Christian polemic, claimed that Syria and Palestine were full of prophets claiming to be gods or to have the power of gods, and preaching salvation (reported by Origen *C. Cels.* 7, 9); it may be that Simon was one of these, and that what is recorded here is a clash between two new religious movements. Later Christian writers make Simon Magus the proto-heretic, and in particular the founder of Gnosticism, a term which covers a number of groups claiming to hold secret knowledge (usually of complex cosmological systems) which would bring salvation to those who held it; they were regarded as a serious threat to orthodox Christianity in the 2nd century. Irenaeus, for example, claims that he was accompanied by a woman called Helen, a reformed prostitute who was, according to Simon, the *Ennoia*, the first thought and the origin of all things; she was now imprisoned in a human body by the powers and angels she had created (one of her past incarnations having been Helen of Troy), and he (Simon) had come to free her and bring salvation to men (*Adv. Haer.* I 23, 2-4). Justin Martyr (*Apol.* I 26, 1-3) claimed to have seen an inscription in Rome honouring Simon as a god (but this may be a misunderstanding of a dedication to *Semo Sancius*, a Roman god responsible for the crops: Dessau no. 3474). He is credited with pupils: Dositheus (Origen *In Joh.* 13, 27) and Menander (Justin *Apol.* I 26, 4; Irenaeus *Adv. Haer.* I 23, 5). All of this sounds very much like later Gnosticism, and whether or not Simon has anything to do with what is credited to him later, it looks as if later generations of Christians remembered him as a much more substantial figure than the magician depicted here.

As it is, he is converted to Christianity, but incurs the condemnation of Peter and John when he offers them money for the purchase of their power to confer the Spirit by laying on hands (v. 19), thereby inventing a new sin, simony, the purchase of ecclesiastical office. Rather than being dismissed with ignominy, or coming to a bad end like Ananias and Sapphira, Simon is made to give a surprisingly dignified reply: **Pray to the Lord for me yourselves and ask that none of the things you have spoken of may fall to me** (v. 24), which suggests that the author of *Acts* believed that Simon remained a Christian.

Philip's next conversion takes place when he is travelling, as instructed by the angel of the Lord (v. 26), on the road from Jerusalem to Gaza. *NEB*'s translation: **This is the desert road** (v. 26) is misleading, as is the punctuation. The literal meaning of the Greek is 'this (feminine) is empty/deserted'; it is not clear whether the sentence is meant as part of the angel's message or as a comment by the author; 'this' could refer to the city of Gaza, which had been destroyed by the Jewish king Alexander Jannaeus early in the 1st century BC and refounded by the proconsul Gabinius in 57 BC on a different site. 'Old' Gaza is described by Greek geographers as 'deserted' (Strabo 16, 759).

On this road he overtakes **a eunuch, a high official of the Kandake, or Queen, of Ethiopia, in charge of all her treasure** (v. 27). In classical Greek (and Roman) authors 'Ethiopian' and 'Ethiopia' are used to refer, not to the peoples and the territory of the modern state of Ethiopia (formerly known in Europe as Abyssinia), but to a people living in the northern part of the modern state of Sudan, and to the Nile valley from the southern frontier of ancient Egypt at Aswan south as far as the area of modern Khartoum. A centralised state, deeply influenced by Egyptian culture, had developed in this area from around 750 BC. It lasted until the fourth century AD and is referred to by modern scholars as Meroe, from the site of its probable capital (see P.L. Shinnie, ch. 4 of the *Cambridge History of Africa*, vol. 2, ed. J.D. Fage). A queen called **Kandake** is referred to as the ruler of the Ethiopians during wars between them and the Roman governors of Egypt in the 20s BC (Strabo 17, 820; Dio Cassius 53, 29; 54, 5), and another such queen is mentioned by the Elder Pliny who reported the information brought back by an exploratory force sent by Nero, and asserted that 'this name has now passed down through the queens for many years' (*Nat. Hist.* 6, 186, cf. 181). Eusebius, retelling this story from *Acts* in his *Ecclesiastical History* (2, 1, 13), claimed (on what basis it is unclear) that it was an ancestral custom for the Ethiopians to be ruled over by a woman 'to this day' (i.e. the early 4th century). An anonymous comment in a Bodleian MS of the New Testament says *á propos* of this verse: 'the Ethiopians call every king's mother Kandake. Thus Bion in the first book of his *Aithiopika*: "the Ethiopians do not make public the fathers of their kings but give it out that they are sons of the sun and they name each mother Kandake" ' (F. Jacoby, *Fr. Griech. Hist.* no. 668, F1). Inscriptions in the Meroitic language (written in scripts derived from the Egyptian ones) confirm that Kandake was a title held from about 250 BC onwards by women of the royal house, but not all holders of the title were ruling queens, who are distinguished, like their male counterparts, by the title *qere*. The reign of one such ruling queen, Amanikhatshan, is dated by one scholar to AD 62-85 (Shinnie in the *Cambridge History of Africa* 2, pp. 230, 248). She may have been the historical person behind the Kandake of the Elder Pliny, and, possibly, of this passage. The *NEB* translation's '*the* Kandake, or Queen, of Ethiopia' implies that the author believed that *Kandake* was the Ethiopic word for queen; no such inference can be drawn from the Greek.

The Ethiopian eunuch **had been to Jerusalem on a pilgrimage** (or, more literally, with *RSV*, **to worship**) (v. 28). There is no other evidence of Jewish settlers or proselytes in Ethiopia, but it is not improbable that they existed, given the fact that there had been Jews in the adjacent region of Upper Egypt since the 5th century BC (a frontier garrison of Jews on the island of Elephantine near Aswan has left a number of papyrus documents: see W.D. Davies and L. Finkelstein, *Cambridge History of Judaism* I, pp. 358-72). For evidence of Jewish presence in Upper Egypt in the first century, see Schürer[2] III (1) pp. 57-8. However, Gentiles did worship at the Temple in Jerusalem; Josephus tells us that at the beginning of the Jewish revolt in AD 66 a decision was taken 'to accept no gift or offering from a foreigner' (*War* 2, 409, 414-16). Strictly speaking, a eunuch could not be a Jew (Deut 23.1), though Isaiah (56.3-5) is much more welcoming to them, as well as to Gentiles. The question of whether he was a Jew or not is avoided by the author, and with it the question of whether the conversion of the eunuch is a precedent for the admission of Gentiles.

Chapter 9

Saul, while travelling to Damascus to persecute Christians there, sees Jesus in a vision, and is converted; he escapes from Damascus, and goes first to Jerusalem, then to Tarsus; Peter heals a paralysed man, and raises a woman from the dead.

The narrative of Saul/Paul's conversion and experiences at Damascus is recapitulated at 22.4-16 and 26.12-20 (in both places the account is put into Paul's own mouth). Paul himself gives accounts of his actions after his conversion in his epistle to the Galatians (1.12-17) and in his second epistle to the Corinthians (11.32-3). The important discrepancies between the accounts in Paul's letters and in *Acts* are as follows: (1) after his conversion, Paul says that he visited Arabia (i.e. the territory of the king of the Nabateans, east of the Jordan) and then 'returned to Damascus' (Gal. 1.17); this visit is not mentioned in *Acts*; (2) Paul stresses that he did not receive the gospel from any man but by direct revelation from Christ (Gal. 1.12), which seems incompatible with the rôle assigned to Ananias in *Acts* (v. 17); (3) the story of Paul being lowered from the walls of Damascus in a basket appears in *2 Corinthians* 11.32 as well as in v. 25 here, but in Paul's version it was not the Jews of Damascus who were watching the gates for his departure, but 'the ethnarch of King Aretas'. This was presumably the result of Paul's earlier visit to Arabia (Gal. 1.17). Kirsopp Lake plausibly argued that the ethnarch was probably having the gates watched from the outside (BC V, pp. 193-4); this hypothesis makes it unnecessary to assume that Damascus was removed from the Roman province of Syria, to the control of Aretas IV of Nabataea, an event which is not otherwise attested (see Schürer[2] I, pp. 581-2).

The differences between the accounts in *Acts* and those in Paul's letters are easily explained in terms of the purposes of the two authors. Paul, especially in *Galatians*, wishes to assert that he is teaching with an independent authority derived directly from God, and is not subordinate to the apostles or the Jerusalem church; so he emphasises that he began his preaching mission immediately on receiving a commission from God (1.16-17); when he went to Jerusalem three years later, he stayed briefly, and spoke only to Peter and James (1.18-20); it was fourteen years before he visited Jerusalem again (2.1). *Acts*, on the other hand, wishes to emphasise the harmony and unity of the church, and in any case the author is always very selective about which episodes he includes; this is not a complete account of everything everyone did, but a selection of relevant episodes.

As in 8.3, it is unclear in what capacity Saul/Paul is travelling to Damascus, and with what authority: **He went to the High Priest and applied for letters to the synagogues at Damascus authorising him to arrest anyone he found, men or women, who followed the new way, and bring them to Jerusalem** (v. 2). That there was a large Jewish settlement in this Gentile city (which had been part of the Roman province of Syria since its occupation by Pompeius' officers in 65 BC: Schürer[2] I, p. 579) is indicated by the large numbers massacred there after the outbreak of the Jewish revolt in AD 66 (according to Josephus in *War* 2, 561, 10,500, or in *War* 7, 368, 18,000). This verse, and the description of the gates of the city being watched in vv. 23-5, could be taken to imply that among the privileges granted by Rome to the organised Jewish communities of the Diaspora were those of arresting dissident Jews and extraditing them to Judaea without consulting the Gentile authorities of the self-governing cities in which they were resident (note that the letters Saul/Paul carries are to the synagogues, not to the local authorities); *Acts* 18.12-16 and *2 Corinthians* 11.24 could be held to show that local synagogues were entitled to have dissidents flogged, and vv. 23-4 that they could even carry out executions. Lake and Cadbury (BC IV, p. 99), followed by Bruce (p. 233), held that one of the privileges of the High Priest (which had been formally confirmed in a pronouncement of Julius Caesar preserved by Josephus, *Ant.* 14, 190-5) was to demand the extradition of Jews. Lake and Cadbury base this claim on a single document in *1 Maccabees* (15.15-24), a circular letter from a Roman consul to Rome's allies in the region, requesting them, among other things, to extradite any 'troublemakers' who had fled from Judaea (v. 21). The revised Schürer[2] (III [1] pp. 119-20) is more circumspect: 'The Jews in fact exercised...a kind of criminal jurisdiction.... Whether they were everywhere formally entitled to do this may be doubted'. In fact, the authenticity of this document is open to very serious challenge (Schürer[2] I, pp. 194-7), and, in any case, a request to client states in the 2nd century BC would not be a good precedent for interference in a city under direct Roman rule two centuries later. The descriptions in *Acts* are quite compatible with unofficial, unauthorised action by loyalist Jews in Damascus; Saul/Paul would 'shanghai' Christians (vv. 1-2), and he himself, later, was simply to be seized and murdered (vv. 23-4: 'watch on the city gates' need not mean an official inspection; it could be done by some tough characters lurking near the gates, ready to grab him and bundle him away through the crowds).

The house in which Saul/Paul stays in Damascus is in **Straight Street** (v. 11), which is traditionally identified with the main east-west road in modern Damascus, called *Derb el-Mustaqim.*

Saul/Paul returns to Jerusalem, where, after some suspicion, he is introduced to the apostles by Barnabas. It is significant that at once he begins **talking and debating with the Greek-speaking Jews** (v. 29). 'Jews' here is an addition by the *NEB* translators, and the *RSV*'s 'Hellenists' is closer to the Greek. The word is the same as that used at 6.1. It seems reasonable to assume that these are not Christians, which makes it more likely that the term in both passages refers to Greek-speaking Hellenised Jews from the Diaspora, but living in Jerusalem. It also confirms the impression that the first reaction against Christianity arose from some sort of dispute within Diaspora Judaism. Saul/Paul himself, the assiduous persecutor of the Christians, and then one of their most active propagandists, would be a Hellenist (he spoke Greek, and came from Tarsus).

The reference to **the church, throughout Judaea, Galilee and Samaria** (v. 31), is puzzling, since elsewhere in *Acts* the word translated 'church', *ekklesia*, usually means the individual local community rather than the church as a whole (see note on 5.11), and surely in this area more than one group of Christians is involved (such as the Samaritans we met at 8.12). Perhaps the author here is still thinking of the Christians in this region as a single community; alternatively, he may be referring only to the Jerusalem church which has been scattered through the region by persecution (8.1).

At this point Peter comes back into the story. He is credited with a healing and a raising from the dead, the point of which is to re-establish him in the narrative as the leader of the community, and to bring him in the direction of Caesarea, in preparation for the momentous events of the next chapter.

Chapter 10

The Gentile Cornelius, prompted by an angel, summons Peter to visit him in Caesarea; on the way, Peter receives a vision, which persuades him to baptise Cornelius.

The admission of Gentiles into the church is perhaps the most significant event in the transformation of Christianity from a Jewish sect to a new religion. It is important to the author of *Acts* that it should be recognised that the first step was taken by Peter, the acknowledged leader of the church, as the result of a direct command from God, rather than by Paul, who will later become the centre of the controversy over this question.

The event takes place **at Caesarea**, and the first unambiguously Gentile convert is **Cornelius, a centurion in the Italian** cohort (v. 1). Caesarea was a new, largely pagan, city founded by Herod I on the Mediterranean coast at a site where he built an artificial harbour; it was dedicated to, and named after the emperor Augustus in 10/9 BC (see Schürer[2] I, p. 306). After the annexation of Judaea in AD 6 it appears to have become the main headquarters of the Roman governor (cf. 23.23-4; 25.6ff.; see Schürer[2] I, p. 361, n. 37 for the evidence of Josephus and Tacitus). It was thus an obvious place for a considerable part of the Roman garrison of the province to be stationed. Before the revolt of 66-70 this garrison consisted of what are called 'auxiliary' units, as distinct from legions. Legions in theory comprised 6,000 men (nearly all infantry) and all of these were Roman citizens; 'auxiliary' units were mainly recruited from subject peoples of the empire without citizenship, and were mostly made up of 500 men (in some cases 1,000). Such units were of two types: 'wings' (Latin *alae*) of cavalry, and 'cohorts' of infantry (each legion was also divided into 10 cohorts). The Greek word *speira* (originally 'coil'; this is the word translated here as 'cohort') which had been applied to a unit of the army of the Ptolemies, had come to be used as the equivalent of the Latin *cohors*. **The Italian Cohort** represents a Greek phrase more literally translated (with *RSV*) as 'what was known as the Italian Cohort', which is a Greek periphrasis for *cohors Italica*. Two units with this title are attested in inscriptions (*cohors I Italica* and *cohors II Italica*), and both are described as *civium Romanorum*, 'of Roman citizens' (something which the description *Italica* would in any case imply). Auxiliary units recruited from Roman citizens in Italy were very much the exception to the general rule. There is evidence that *cohors II Italica* was stationed in Syria in AD 69 (Schürer[2] I, p. 365, n. 54; cf. BC V, pp. 441-2), but no other evidence that it was ever in Judaea; so there is controversy about the accuracy of this report in *Acts* (Schürer[2], loc. cit.).

In Greek, Cornelius is described as a *hekatontarches*, 'commander of a hundred', the normal Greek translation of the Latin *centurio*. These men were the equivalent of senior NCOs in the British army, usually (but not always) promoted from the ranks, whereas their superiors (the prefects in overall command of the auxiliary 'cohorts' and the 'tribunes' of the legions) were usually appointed directly from civilian life, from men of high rank. Each cohort was commanded by a single prefect with several centurions under him.

Cornelius has a Latin name, one of the most common of Roman 'clan-names', but that need not mean that he was a Roman citizen; indeed the absence of a 'family name' to distinguish him from numerous other Cornelii is rather suspicious (contrast Claudius Lysias in 23.26, who *was* a Roman citizen [22.28]; see Introduction pp. 25-6; Sherwin-White [1963] pp. 156 and 160-1). However, if he had been promoted from the ranks of a cohort of Roman citizens (rather than transferred from an ordinary cohort), he would in fact have been a citizen.

NEB's **He was a religious man, and he and his whole family joined in the worship of God** (v. 2) is more precisely translated by *RSV* **as a devout man who feared God with all his household**. *RSV*'s 'household' is a less misleading translation of the Greek *oikos* than the *NEB*'s 'family' (see note on 16.15). Later (v. 22) Cornelius is described as **a good and religious man, acknowledged as such by the whole Jewish nation**. What is more **he gave generously to help the Jewish people, and was regular in his prayers to God** (v. 2). Cornelius must then have been a 'god-fearer', one of those Gentiles who joined in synagogue worship, and adopted some Jewish practices (see e.g. Juvenal, *Satires* 14, 96-106, for a Gentile sympathiser who keeps the Sabbath and has given up idol-worship and pork), but did not go as far as circumcision or adopting the whole Jewish dietary law (see Introduction p. 21). Cornelius is still a Gentile (and Peter naturally anticipates that his household, in Jewish terms, cannot be guaranteed to be ritually clean). The soldier who is sent to Peter as a messenger, and who is described as **a religious man** (v. 8), was presumably another 'god-fearer'.

The vision which Peter receives in anticipation of the arrival of Cornelius' summons is ostensibly concerned with the Jewish food laws. The basic rules are laid out in *Leviticus* (see esp. ch. 11) and prohibit the eating of a range of animals, of which pigs are only the best known. Later interpretation had built on these a comprehensive body of rules designed to exclude even the possibility of incurring pollution by association with what was unclean (see Schürer[2] II, pp. 83-4). As a consequence it was impossible for any Jew who wished to remain within the law to eat Gentile food or eat with Gentiles, and very difficult even to enter a Gentile home (cf. Tacitus, *Hist.* 5, 5, on the Jews: *separati epulis*, 'they eat by themselves'). So whatever was included in the **creatures of every kind, whatever walks or crawls or flies** (v. 12) contained in the sheet Peter is shown in his vision, and which he is commanded to **kill and eat** (v. 13), it is a certainty that defining them all as pure (v. 15) constitutes an abrogation of the food laws which Peter will have kept all his life (v. 16). Certainly he immediately interprets the vision as permission to associate with, and enter the household of, Gentiles (vv. 28-9), rather than to admit them to the Christian community. It is only when, while Peter was preaching to them, **the Holy Spirit came upon all who were listening** (v. 44) that the decision is taken that they cannot be refused baptism. In other words, Gentiles are admitted not just on the strength of Peter's interpretation of his vision, but as a consequence of a direct intervention of God; in this case (unlike that of the Samaritans of 8.5-17) baptism comes *after* the gift of the Spirit. The coming of the Holy Spirit is marked here by **speaking in tongues** (v. 46), which sounds much closer to the ecstatic but incomprehensible utterances which Paul met in Corinth than to the experience at Pentecost (see notes on 2.1-12).

Chapter 11

News of the Gentile converts is brought to Jerusalem; the message spreads both to Jews and Gentiles beyond Palestine, and especially to Antioch; Agabus predicts famine, and a relief fund is started.

It is interesting that when Peter reports **to the apostles and the members of the church in Judaea that Gentiles too had accepted the word of God** (v. 1), the question they raise with him concerns not admission to the community, but simply associating with Gentiles: **You have been visiting men who are uncircumcised...and sitting at table with them!** (v. 3). When Peter relates his vision, and tells of the gift of the Holy Spirit, **their doubts were silenced** (v. 18), but not, in view of what happens later (see ch. 15, and cf. what Paul says in *Galatians* 2.11-21), permanently.

The author now turns his attention to the spread of the Christian message by the scattered Jerusalem church first **to Jews only** (v. 19) in **Phoenicia, Cyprus, and Antioch** (for Jewish settlements in these places, see Schürer² III [1] pp. 13, 15, 68), but then, through **natives of Cyprus and Cyrene** (v. 20; presumably they are 'Hellenists' from Jerusalem) to pagans also, in Antioch on the Orontes, the largest city in the empire after Rome and Alexandria. It was founded in 300 BC by Seleucus I and named after his father Antiochus; it became the virtual capital of the kingdom of the Seleucids. Josephus (*War* 7, 45) reports that there was an exceptionally large Jewish community there, who 'were attracting to their worship a great number of Greeks, making them virtually members of their own community'. The author of *Acts* seems to have had a special interest in Antioch, which is probably the reason why he is sometimes said to have been an Antiochene. The intriguing report that **it was in Antioch that the**

disciples first got the name of Christians (v. 26) may mean that for the first time they are being recognised as a group distinct from the mainstream Jews. The Greek word *Christos* is simply the standard Septuagint translation of the Hebrew *mashiah*, 'the anointed one'. The term was originally applied to the king of Israel and alludes to the ceremony of anointing as a sign of accession to the kingship (e.g. 1 Sam. 9.16). It could also be applied to others with a commission from God, such as the prophet Elisha (1 Kings 19.16), and on one occasion (Isa. 45.1) it is used of the Persian king Cyrus (presumably as the appointed agent of God). After the extinction of the Jewish kingdoms, the hope that there would again be a true king of Israel, an 'anointed one', was kept alive, but gradually becomes involved with apocalyptic expectations, where the appearance of the *mashiah* heralds the end of the present age. (Schürer[2] II, pp. 488-554; O. Cullman, *The Christology of the New Testament*, pp. 111-17). The significance of the application of the term *Christos* to Jesus is a matter of acute theological controversy. In any case, the term would be meaningless to a non-Jewish Greek speaker. When, in the 2nd century, the Hebrew scriptures were again translated into Greek by Aquila and by Theodotion, *Christos* is replaced by *Aleimennos* (which also means 'the anointed one'), presumably because by that time *Christos* had been appropriated by the Christians.

The **prophets** who **came down from Jerusalem** (v. 27) will have been men (or perhaps women, as in the case of Philip's prophetic daughters at 21.9) who claimed to speak for God. This need not involve predicting the future, but one of them, Agabus, (who appears also at 21.10) did **predict a severe and world-wide famine, which in fact occurred in the reign of Claudius** (v. 28). If this statement is interpreted strictly, Agabus' prophecy must have been made before the accession of Claudius in AD 41; the next episode in *Acts*, however, must have taken place after AD 41 (see note on 12.1, and Introduction p. 31 on the chronology of *Acts*). The assertion about a world-wide famine is an exaggeration. Josephus describes a 'great famine' at Jerusalem (after the death of Herod Agrippa I in 44, during the resumed rule of Roman governors: *Ant.* 20, 51 and 101); hence the relief to be sent to Judaea (v. 29). Dio Cassius (60, 11) records a food shortage at Rome in AD 41 and Tacitus another in AD 51 (*Annals* 12, 43), but they do not specify in which of the several areas which supplied the capital (Sicily, Africa, Egypt) the crops had failed. Suetonius' reference to 'repeated crop failures' (*Claudius* 18, 2) is also imprecise. The general conclusion of a recent study is that the normal pattern in classical antiquity was not one of large-scale famines leading to mass starvation but one of frequent local food shortages (P. Garnsey, *Famine and Food Supply in the Graeco-Roman World*, pp. 37-9). Collections for the relief of Palestine are mentioned also by Paul in his letter to the Romans (15.25-7), and in *Galatians*

(2.10) he reports a request for assistance from James, Peter, and John: 'All they asked was that we should keep their poor in mind, which was the very thing I made it my business to do'. All male Jews over the age of 20 (even those of the Diaspora) were obliged to make a contribution of half a shekel (later two drachmas) to maintain the sacrifices at the Temple at Jerusalem. Perhaps these relief collections, specifically for the church in Judaea, were thought of as an equivalent for Gentile converts, a means of showing their allegiance to the community at the heart of their religion. The contribution is to be sent to **the elders** (v. 30), who appear here for the first time. They are not the same as the apostles (see 15.2). In *Galatians* Paul refers to 'those reputed pillars of our society, James, Cephas, and John' (2.9), who seem to form an authoritative but informal group, and perhaps this sort of group is meant here, rather than a distinct class of officers such as developed later.

Chapter 12

Herod kills James and arrests Peter; an angel releases Peter from prison; Herod dies at Caesarea.

King Herod (v. 1) is usually referred to in modern works as Herod Agrippa I (his official Roman name was Marcus Iulius Agrippa). He was the son of Aristoboulos, one of the two sons of Herod the Great (both executed by their father) and Mariamne the Hasmonean, and was named Agrippa after his grandfather's main Roman protector, Marcus Agrippa, son-in-law of Augustus. Herod Agrippa (born in 10 BC) was brought up in Rome alongside younger members of Augustus' family, and was eventually able to use his influence with them to become ruler of most of his grandfather's territories; in AD 37 the new emperor Gaius gave him the title king and the territories formerly ruled by his uncle Philip (died in 33/34), to which were added in 39 or 40 Galilee and Peraea, which had been ruled by another uncle, Antipas, until his banishment. In early 41 Agrippa was in Rome when Gaius was assassinated and helped to ensure the succession of Gaius' uncle Claudius, for which he was rewarded by the inclusion of the entire province of Judaea in his kingdom (see Schürer[2] I, pp. 442-5).

We are not told why Herod abruptly intervenes at this point, or what sequence of events led to the point when he **beheaded James, the brother of John** (v. 2). Decapitation with a sword (and the Greek text says explicitly that James was killed with a sword) was a form of execution regularly inflicted on provincials by Roman governors. Agrippa was clearly adopting Roman forms of government. There is no question in this case of a lynching, as in the case of Stephen. The statement that this was a popular move (**he saw that the Jews approved** v. 2; see also v. 11) is in marked contrast to reports in the earlier chapters of *Acts* of the high regard in which the Christians were held by the people of Jerusalem (e.g. 4.21; 4.33; 5.26); the unrelenting hostility of the Jews is a recurring feature of the narrative in the rest of *Acts*.

Herod Agrippa's adoption of Roman procedures is shown also when Peter, having been arrested, is put **under a military guard, four squads of four men each** (v. 4); (the Greek word used here for the squads is *tetradia*, which comes from a root meaning 'made up of four'; Jerome translates it into Latin by *quaternis*). The Latin writer on Roman military affairs, Vegetius, records that it was standard practice in the Roman army for guard duty at night to be carried out by groups of four (*quaterni*: *De Re Militari* 3, 8; that this dates back to at least the 2nd century BC is shown by Polybius 6, 33, 7). Philo of Alexandria uses *tetradia* as a shorthand for 'watch-duty' (*In Flaccum* 111). The reasoning in this case behind assigning four such squads of four is given by Vegetius (loc. cit.): 'and because it was considered impossible for individuals to remain watchful at the look-outs, the watches were divided into four parts by the water-clock in order that it should not be necessary to keep watch for longer than three hours of the night'. In fact these soldiers were probably drawn from some of the auxiliary cohorts which had previously served under the Roman prefects and remained in Judaea under Agrippa: see Schürer[2] I, p. 363.

The story of Peter's imprisonment and release by an angel looks suspiciously like a repeat of 5.17-21, but this time the story has much more circumstantial detail (e.g. v. 15) and is told with considerably greater narrative skill. The author must feel that he has better and fuller sources for this event than for the previous incident. **John Mark** (v. 12) (*RSV*'s 'John whose other name was Mark' represents the Greek better) is a case of a Roman name being applied to a non-citizen; Marcus is one of the short list of personal names given to Roman boys, and any citizen would be distinguished by his 'clan-name' (see Introduction pp. 25-6). This is the last episode in *Acts* where any story about Peter, or indeed any of the apostles, is told for its own sake. For the rest of the book they are brought in only when what they do has some bearing on Paul or his work.

The death of Herod Agrippa I is also described by Josephus (*Ant.* 19, 343-52), and his version has significant points of agreement with, and differences from, that of *Acts*. The main similarities are that Herod Agrippa (i) wears special dress, (ii) accepts acclamations as a god, (iii) dies after a sudden attack of illness, and (iv) all this happens at Caesarea. The significant differences are that in the account of Josephus (i) it is not on the occasion of an address to a deputation from Tyre and Sidon, but at the celebration of a pagan festival that he puts on his robes, and (ii) it is not **the populace** (v. 22) but flatterers among office-holders and men of rank who acclaim him as a god. Josephus' account is longer with a number of additional details: a description of the robe woven with silver, and the omen of an owl perched over Herod Agrippa's head. According to Josephus (*Ant.* 19, 343) he died after completing three full years of rule over Judaea, i.e. in AD 44 (Schürer[2] I, p. 452, n. 43). There are problems over accepting the claim in *Acts* that the occasion of the incident arose because **he had for some time been furiously angry with the people of Tyre and Sidon** (v. 20), who had decided to sue for peace **because their country drew its supplies from the king's territory** (v. 20), which suggests that he had banned, or threatened to ban, the export of grain to these cities. Tyre and Sidon lay in the Roman province of Syria. Given that Roman governors were very concerned to forestall disturbances in large towns, and hence were concerned also about the food supply to such towns, this would be a bold step for Herod Agrippa, as a Roman appointee, to take, even if he was a favourite of the emperor's. In this case Josephus' account is more plausible. The title of the **royal chamberlain** (v. 20) means literally 'the one in charge of the king's bedroom'. The title is used of a high official in the Seleucid court in the 2nd century BC. The **rostrum** (v. 21) on which the king sits (in Greek *bema*) is a platform from which a speaker addressed a political assembly or a court, and the word is also used as the equivalent of the Latin *tribunal*, the elevated platform from which Roman officials (themselves seated) administered justice or received deputations. Once again, Herod Agrippa has adopted Roman procedure.

Chapter 13

Barnabas and Saul are commissioned by the Spirit to travel spreading the word; in Cyprus they defeat a magician and convert the governor; in Pisidian Antioch they are driven out as a result of a persecution instigated by the Jews.

The chapter begins with a list of **prophets and teachers** (v. 1). Prophets we have met already (11.27); teachers in *Acts*, as in the epistles (e.g. 1 Tim. 2.7), seem to be simply preachers, although in *Ephesians* (4.11) they are distinguished from evangelists. In the next generation their function had become sufficiently formalised for the author of the *Epistle of Barnabas* to wish to distinguish himself from them: 'I am going to explain to you a few things, not as a teacher, but as one of yourselves' (1, 8). Of those mentioned by name, we have met **Barnabas** already. The first name of **Simeon called Niger** is a common Hebrew name, and his alternative name, which is the Latin for 'black', is probably just a distinguishing nickname (Niger is used as a *cognomen*, but a single Latin name is not proof of Roman citizen status: see Introduction p. 26). **Lucius of Cyrene** has a very common Roman *praenomen* (occasionally found as a *gentilicium* or as a *cognomen*), but on its own this is no proof of Roman citizen status; he was clearly a Jew whose family had resided in Cyrene, like the Simon who was ordered to carry the cross in Jesus' place (Mark 15.21), but it is unlikely that he was a citizen of the *polis* of Cyrene, which had strict rules about the qualification for citizenship (see S. Applebaum, *Jews and Greeks in Ancient Cyrene* pp. 175-90); Jews from Cyrene and Cyprus (like Barnabas) had founded the church in Antioch (11.20). **Manaen,** we are told, **had been at the court of Prince Herod.** 'Prince' here is more literally translated (with *RSV*) 'tetrarch'; this must be Herod Antipas, the youngest son of Herod I, who had ruled Galilee and Peraea from his father's death until his deposition and banishment to Gaul by the emperor Gaius in 39; he is described in Greek as Herod's *syntrophos* (= foster-brother), which in its literal meaning would signify that they were brought up together, but here probably means simply that he was a royal courtier; at the courts of Hellenistic kings 'foster-brother', like 'kinsman', had come to be a title of honour, and the relationship to the king could be a fictitious one.

The words the Spirit (speaking presumably through one of the prophets) uses to commission Barnabas and Saul, **Set Barnabas and Saul apart for me** (v. 2), are in Greek probably a deliberate reminiscence of terms used in the Septuagint in similar circumstances (e.g. Lev. 20.25 of clean and unclean animals; Num. 8.11 of the Levites); Paul himself uses the expression of his own mission (Rom. 1.1; Gal. 1.15).

They sail from **Seleucia** (v. 4), a city in Pieria, near the mouth of the Orontes, one of four *poleis* founded in north Syria by Seleucus I, and named after himself. This is the first of many sea voyages undertaken by Paul in *Acts*; he himself (2 Cor. 11.25) refers to being shipwrecked three times and spending a day and night adrift in the open sea. Of course their destination, Cyprus, could only be reached by ship, but it was in any case quicker and easier to travel by water than overland in ancient times. The apparent ease with which sea passages could be obtained is remarkable; the evidence of underwater archaeology indicates that sea traffic on the Mediterranean reached an intensity in the 1st and 2nd centuries not to be equalled until the 14th century: see K. Hopkins, *JRS* 70 (1980).

They arrive at **Salamis** (v. 5), an ancient Greek *polis* on the east coast of the island, the nearest port to Seleucia, and proceed to begin their teaching **in the Jewish synagogues.** There were flourishing communities of Jews on the island (Josephus, *Ant.* 13, 284-7; Philo. *Leg.* 282); after 420,000 people allegedly died on Cyprus in the Jewish revolt ca. 115-17 Jews were forbidden to land on the island (Dio Cassius 58, 32, 3). A **synagogue** is an 'assembly' or 'congregation'; the word came to be used for the place where the Jews in a particular city assembled for prayer and the study of the scriptures, although the older word for the place of assembly was *proseuche*, 'place of prayer' (cf. 16.13, 16; it is used in inscribed dedications of 'synagogues' in Egypt in the 3rd century BC). The **John** who goes with them **as their assistant** (v. 5) is presumably the John Mark of 12.25. He is probably to be identified with the Marcus described as Barnabas' cousin in *Colossians* 4.10. The precise meaning of the word translated 'assistant' is unclear; Luke's gospel uses the word of a synagogue servant (4.20) and in the phrase 'servants of the gospel' (1.2).

Paphos is on the west coast of Cyprus, hence they must travel **through the whole island** (v. 6) to get there. There were two sites at Paphos: Old Paphos, with a famous temple of Aphrodite who, according to one version of the myth, had risen from the foam off this coast; and New Paphos, founded by the last native king of the city, Nicocles II (deposed 306 BC). Under Roman rule Paphos enjoyed the title *metropolis* (= mother-city) of the province, but this is merely a recognition of a higher rank than the other cities, and not proof that Paphos was a 'capital' in the modern sense (i.e. the seat of government), since our knowledge of the practice of other proconsuls makes it unlikely that the proconsul of Cyprus was permanently resident in one city. There is no way of telling where the encounter described in the next few verses took place; the 'there' in *NEB*'s **there they came upon a sorcerer, a Jew who posed as a prophet, Bar-Jesus by name** (v. 6) represents nothing in the Greek. This 'sorcerer' is in fact a *magos*, like Simon (8.11). The name he is given, Bar-Jesus, is a Greek transliteration from the Aramaic of the man's patronymic, 'son of Jesus' (= Joshua); there is no significance in the name; Jesus is a common enough name, and we find another in Col. 4.10. He is represented as being, as well as a *magos*, a false prophet, i.e. one who falsely claims to be the messenger of God. Warnings against 'false prophets' appear as early as *Deuteronomy* (18.20); similar warnings are attributed to Jesus (Mark 13.22; Matt. 24.24); in the next generation a warning against the false prophet 'who corrupts the mind of the servants of God' is found in *The Shepherd of Hermas* (Mand. 11). Jews were forbidden to practise as magicians (see Deut 18.10-14). Nevertheless, Pliny (*Nat. Hist.* 30, 11) associates Jews with magic, as does Lucian (*Podagra* 173). The *Didache*, a manual of church discipline produced in the next generation, must still repeat the prohibition of sorcery: 'you must not practise sorcery' (2, 2). How **the Governor, Sergius Paulus** (v. 7) came to hear of Paul and Barnabas we are not told, but a man who included in his entourage a *magos* and prophet (even a false one) must be presumed to have had a well-known interest in religion (compare the emperor Tiberius and his astrologer Thrasyllus; also, in the late 2nd century a senior senator, Rutilianus, was, according to Lucian [*Alex.* 30-5, 48], hoodwinked by a charlatan named Alexander and his new god in the form of a long-haired snake). The governor has the title *anthu-patos* (= proconsul): see Introduction p. 25. Cyprus had been annexed in 58 BC after the suicide of the junior member of the Ptolemy dynasty who was its last king, and since 22 BC had been a separate province, governed by proconsuls chosen by lot from ex-praetors, and replaced annually. There was a Sergius Paulus family in the ranks of the Roman Senate in the 1st and 2nd centuries. Although no other direct evidence has appeared of this man's term of office in Cyprus, a L. Sergius Paulus, who served as a member of the board of five senators who had charge of the bed and banks of the Tiber in the reign of Claudius, would have been of the right seniority at the right period.

The phrase: **Elymas the sorcerer (so his name may be translated)...** (v. 8) is very difficult to interpret. Since we have been told at 13.6 that the sorcerer's name is Bar-Jesus, it should mean that 'Elymas the sorcerer' is a translation of Bar-Jesus, which is impossible, since Bar-Jesus seems to have no meaning which can have anything to do with the supposed translation, and Elymas itself is a word which would mean nothing to a Greek-speaking reader, and so it would be useless as a translation. The meaning must be that *magos* is a translation of Elymas, a name not otherwise known, and whose meaning remains obscure. The suggestion that it is derived from the Arabic root *elim* (= wise) would explain the translation as *magos*, but it is not easy to see how a Cypriot Jew might have come by an Arabic name. If, instead of Elymas, we were to adopt the reading of the 'Western' text, *Hetoimas*, the name might be taken as a derivative of the word *Hetoimos* (= ready) but this would remain an unlikely translation of either *magos* or Bar-Jesus. Josephus (*Ant.* 20, 142) mentions a magician called Atomos, also a Jew from Cyprus, as being active at about this period. The relationship of this Atomos to Elymas (or indeed Hetoimas) is a matter for speculation. For a full discussion of this problem, see the notes of Bruce and Haenchen on this verse.

The attempts of Elymas **to turn the Governor away from the Faith** (v. 8) (or 'from faith'; the Greek word *pistis* used here can mean either belief in the subjective sense or the Faith, i.e. Christianity) are opposed vigorously by Saul, who, we are now told for the first time in *Acts*, was **also known as Paul** (v. 9). From this point onwards he is invariably referred to by his Latin name; no explanation why is offered; for Paul's names as a Roman see Introduction p. 26. Paul responds to Elymas with a speech (vv. 10-11) composed almost entirely of phrases taken from the Septuagint. **Son of the devil** (v. 10) is not, of course, to be taken literally. In Hebrew, phrases of the form 'son of x' are quite a common way of expressing the idea of 'a man with the quality x'. Such phrases are literally translated into the Greek of the Septuagint, and are imitated by New Testament writers. 'Devil' represents the Greek *diabolos* (literally 'slanderer'), which itself is a translation of the Hebrew *satan* (= the adversary, perhaps in the sense of a prosecutor in a law-court). In the Old Testament it is used either in a very general sense (e.g. 1 Chron. 21.1; 1 Macc. 1.36) or in the sense of the accuser of men before God (see especially Job 1.6 and *passim*), in which rôle Satan seems to be part of the court of heaven. In the New Testament, however, he has his own kingdom (Matt. 12.26), his own angels (Matt. 25.41), and his own followers (1 John 3.8-10). It has been suggested that the picture of the *diabolos* found in the New Testament (and in Jewish apocryphal writings) may have been influenced by the religion of the Persians, Zoroastrianism, which was dualistic in character. The Zoroastrian god, Ahuramazda, was opposed by an evil adversary, Angra Mainyu; each was supported by a host of angelic and demonic powers, who were engaged in waging a constant cosmic war (W.D. Davies and L. Finkelstein, *The Cambridge History of Judaism* I, pp. 315-18). *Acts* uses both *diabolos* and *Satanas* (e.g. 5.3) without apparent distinction in meaning.

Elymas is struck blind, and the Governor, **deeply impressed** (v. 12), becomes a believer. He is not, however, baptised, nor does he receive the gift of the Spirit.

Leaving Paphos, Paul and his companions went by sea to Perga in Pamphylia (v. 13), though, since Perge is inland, the landing was probably at Attaleia (modern Antalya), from which they leave in 14.25. The district of Pamphylia was a narrow coastal plain bounded by the mountainous regions of Lycia to the west and Cilicia to the east, and was the nearest part of the Asian mainland to Paphos. At this point John Mark leaves them (see 15.37-9). Paul and Barnabas then **continued their journey as far as Pisidian Antioch** (v. 14) which would mean that they had to pass through the regions of Pisidia and Isauria, a triangle of harsh mountainous territory. The mountain tribes had long preyed on travellers and fiercely resisted external powers. King Amyntas of Galatia had been killed in 25 BC, and Roman campaigns in 10-5 BC had been followed by the plantation of Roman colonies to the north of the mountains (see Introduction p. 16). It was here, if anywhere on his travels, that Paul would have been likely to face the dangers from bandits mentioned in *2 Corinthians* 11.26. The correct form of the name Pisidian Antioch was Antioch-next-to-Pisidia (Strabo. 12, 569). The city in fact lay north of the area where Pisidian had been spoken, and was in that part of the Phrygian-speaking region included in the province of Galatia (see Introduction p. 23). This Antioch was the site of a great shrine of a native Anatolian moon god, *Men*, and must have been renamed after Antiochus I or II after the territory came under Seleucid rule in 281 BC. It was the site of the most important of the Roman colonies founded in the area under Augustus.

The synagogue service which Paul and Barnabas attend in Pisidian

Antioch (v. 15) begins (as always) with a reading from the *Torah* (the first five books of the Bible), and (as often, but not inevitably) from the Prophets (which included Joshua, Judges, and the books of Samuel and Kings as well as the more obvious prophetical books). They then receive a message from **the officials of the synagogue** (v. 15), inviting them to address the congregation. An *archisynagogus* (= leader of the synagogue) seems to have been the member of the congregation responsible for the maintenance of the building and the arrangements for holding services. Normally there seems to have been only one *archisynagogus* (see 18.8). The plural occurs in only one other place in the New Testament (Mark 5.22; the parallel passage in Luke 8.41 changes the term to the Greek singular, *archon tes synagoges*). There is evidence that in some cases the title may have been simply honorific, and could be given to women or children. Any member of the congregation could be invited to give the address, and it is not surprising that the *archisynagogos* was responsible for issuing the invitation (see Schürer[2] II, pp. 434ff., III [1] pp. 100-1).

Paul's speech (vv. 16-41), his first substantial speech recorded in *Acts*, is perhaps intended to be representative of his approach to preaching to Jews, in the same way as his speech at Athens (17.22-31) represents his approach to a Gentile audience. The coming of Jesus as Messiah is presented as the culmination of God's dealings with the Jewish people, the fulfilment of his promises. A brief account of Jewish history is given (rather cursorily since the readers of *Acts* will already have seen it laid out in detail in Stephen's speech at 7.2-53). The Jews' rejection of Jesus is represented as being due to ignorance (13.27) rather than wickedness, and the Roman authorities, as usual in *Acts*, are exonerated from blame (13.28). Paul then tells of the appearance of the risen Jesus to many witnesses as evidence that he is the fulfilment of the promises made by God to the Jews, and backs up the argument by the exposition of passages selected from the Old Testament. The speech concludes with the promise of forgiveness of sins to those who believe, and a threat to those who do not.

Paul's speech is addressed to **you who worship our God** (v. 16), as well as to the Jews in the congregation. Presumably these people (in Greek *phoboumenoi ton theon*) are non-Jewish 'god-fearers' like Cornelius (10.2). They appear among those who welcome Paul's message (v. 43) as **Gentile worshippers**. The Greek behind this phrase is *sebomenon proselyton*, 'god-fearing proselytes', an odd and puzzling expression only found here. Proselytes are strictly speaking Gentiles who have become full converts to Judaism, having undergone circumcision (if male) and adopted the Jewish dietary laws in their entirety. 'God-fearers' on the other hand are, like Cornelius, usually Gentiles who attend the synagogue, who may have adopted certain Jewish practices but who have not become Jews by conversion.

The **persecution** (v. 50) which is stirred up against Paul and Barnabas is described in very vague terms. The moving force is the Jews, inspired by **jealous resentment** (v. 45; presumably at the success of the Christians among actual and potential 'god-fearers'); they act through **the women of standing who were worshippers** and **the leading men of the city** (v. 50). The women, 'god-fearers', are described by the Greek word *euschemonas*, which means originally 'elegant' or 'refined', but comes to denote high social position; the word is applied to Joseph of Arimathea in *Mark* (15.43), but the parallel passage of *Matthew* substitutes *plousios*, 'rich', so perhaps that is the meaning here; the same phrase occurs at 17.12. The **leading men of the city**, however (who, perhaps significantly, are not said to be 'god-fearers') represent, if not the local magistrates themselves, then at least the class from which the magistrates were drawn. It looks as if what may be happening is not just an ordinary riot but action by the authorities. The author, always anxious to emphasise that the early Christians were entirely law-abiding, and no threat to public order, rather glosses over the details, but leaves us in no doubt that in his view the root cause of the disturbances was Jewish jealousy. Paul and Barnabas leave after shaking the dust off their feet, a gesture of rejection enjoined upon his disciples by Jesus himself (Mark 6.11; Matt. 10.14; Luke 10.11).

Chapter 14

Paul and Barnabas are driven from Iconium; they heal a cripple at Lystra, and narrowly escape being honoured as gods; Paul is stoned; after other travels, they return to Antioch.

The next town visited is **Iconium**, (v. 1) (modern Konya), separated from Antioch by the range now known as Sultan Dagh; it was situated on the eastern side of the mountain, on the great east-west road along the southern edge of the Anatolian plateau, which ran west from the Cilician Gates towards the Aegean. It had become the site of a Roman colony under Augustus, but a Hellenised *polis* continued in existence on the same site (see Introduction p. 16). All classical writers later than Xenophon (ca. 400 BC) describe Iconium as lying in Lycaonia; the archaeological and epigraphic evidence, on the other hand, indicates that Iconium lay within the area of Phrygian speech and culture. Apart from the mention of the synagogue here, there is no other direct evidence for Jewish settlement in Iconium.

The visit begins well, with **a large body both of Jews and Gentiles** (or, as *RSV* more literally translates, **Greeks**; v. 1) accepting the message, but trouble is soon stirred up by **unconverted Jews** (v. 2); presumably the author uses the word 'unconverted' to remind us that at this stage not all Jews were hostile, and many were becoming believers. The dispute comes to a head when **a move was made by Gentiles and Jews together, with the connivance of the city authorities, to maltreat them and stone them** (v. 5). 'City authorities' here translates the Greek word *archontes* (= leaders or rulers), and it may be that what is referred to is not the elected *archons* of the *polis*, but simply the leaders of the synagogue. In any case, the mention of stoning suggests that this is a case of 'unofficial' mob violence, rather than action by the civic authorities. But it is not clear whether there was official connivance here, as there was in Thessalonica (17.6).

In the course of this episode, Paul and Barnabas are referred to as **apostles** (v. 4); the title is repeated at v. 14, but is used elsewhere in *Acts* only of the Twelve (see note on 1.21-2). There is no obvious reason why the term should be used here, and only here. It seems to be simply an oversight, and suggests that the author was aware that Paul (and perhaps others also) called themselves apostles, and that his decision to restrict the title to the Twelve is a deliberate one. In the next generation, the term is used in the *Didache* (11, 3-6) in the more general sense.

They **made their escape to the Lycaonian cities of Lystra and Derbe and the surrounding country** (v. 6); both places lay to the south-east of Iconium, along the route which ran east from Iconium to the Cilician Gates, the pass through the Taurus range beyond which lay Tarsus. Lystra was the site of a third Augustan colony, (see Introduction p. 16), but it was not a major town. Nor was Derbe, the only one of the four cities evangelised on this journey which was not the site of an Augustan colony; even its site was not identified until the 1950s. Lycaonia was the name of the region in southern Anatolia where the Lycaonian language was spoken in the Greco-Roman period (still in use in Paul's day: v. 11). Lycaonia had been part of the Roman province of Galatia since its formation in 25 BC, but part of the region had been bestowed by the emperor Gaius on his friend King Antiochus IV of Commagene; Lystra and Derbe remained in the province of Galatia. The 'surrounding country' presumably refers to the countryside included in the political 'territories' of the two cities. This is the only direct reference in *Acts* to Paul visiting the countryside on his missionary journeys (but see 16.6-8). See Introduction p. 20 for the cultural and linguistic differences between *polis* and *chora* which make it unlikely that the visit had evangelisation for its purpose; presumably the motive was to evade the pursuing Jews of Iconium (and Antioch: v. 19). The wording of the phrase seems to suggest that both *polis* and *chora* were included in their evangelisation, but it is unlikely that much could have been achieved in the *chora*.

On arrival at Lystra, Paul heals a lame man, with the result that the people **shouted in their native Lycaonian, 'The gods have come down to us in human form'** (v. 11). This is the only reference in *Acts* to any native vernacular being used outside Judaea (see 22.2). One would assume from *Acts* that all evangelisation and conversation was carried on in Greek. Nor is there any reference to Latin either at Rome (ch. 28) or in the Roman colonies such as Lystra itself; but Latin probably only survived as a language for official business in the colonies founded in the eastern provinces, and as for Rome itself, not only does Paul write to the church there in Greek (*Romans*), but also Christians in Rome were writing in Greek well into the 2nd century (e.g. *The Shepherd of Hermas*, completed, according to the Muratorian canon, about the middle of the 2nd century). The reason for the reference to the Lycaonian language here must be to explain why Paul and Barnabas did not react immediately to this acclamation as they did later (v. 14); they could not understand the shouts, and not until they saw the preparations for a pagan sacrifice did they understand how they were being honoured. Yet clearly the people in Lystra and the surrounding area did understand and speak Greek; evangelisation is possible (v. 7), and Paul is understood by the lame man (v. 9) and the crowd (v. 18). It is entirely plausible that the masses in such a city would be bilingual, but have recourse to the local vernacular in moments of excitement.

It has been argued that the population of Lystra would be inclined to jump to this conclusion, and to identify a pair of supposedly supernatural visitors with the Greek gods Zeus and Hermes (v. 12: *NEB* uses anglicised forms of the Latin equivalents **Jupiter** and **Mercury**) because of a well-known local legend of an aged couple who had entertained Zeus and Hermes in human guise. This is the story of Baucis and Philemon, retold by Ovid in his *Metamorphoses* (8, 620-724), and set by him in Phrygia. There seems, however, to be no firm evidence of Ovid's source for the story, so there is no certainty at all that such a legend was current in the 1st century in Lycaonia. Epigraphic evidence from the 3rd century which couples the names of Zeus and Hermes proves nothing (see Bruce, pp. 321-2 for references; see also A.S. Hollis' edition of *Metamorphoses VIII*, pp. 106-12). The fact that they called Paul **Mercury, because he was the spokesman** (v. 12) suggests that the Lystrans are referring to the Greek gods specifically in their Greek characters, and not to local Lycaonian gods which had been identified with Zeus and Hermes (as was argued in, e.g. BC IV p. 164). One of the functions attributed to Hermes in Greek religion, as early as the Homeric poems, was that of the herald who spoke on behalf of the other gods (for which reason he became the patron of oratory).

The sacrifice is prepared by **the priest of Jupiter, whose temple was just outside the city** (v. 13), or, more literally 'the priest of Zeus who was in front of the city'. Greek gods were worshipped with a variety of additional epithets: *proastios* ('before the town', 'suburban') is recorded on an inscription from Claudiopolis (not far from Lystra) as an epithet of Zeus, and *propolis* ('before the city') is also found as an epithet of Dionysos. For the sacrifice, he brings **oxen and garlands to the gates** (v. 13), although the oxen are actually bulls (Greek *taurous*), uncastrated male victims being appropriate in a sacrifice to male gods. It was customary in classical religion to 'dress up' sacrificial victims; the Greek word translated 'garlands', *stemmata*, derives from the verb *stephein*, 'to put around, to crown', and such 'wreaths' could take the form of woollen fillets as well as garlands of flowers. The Greek word translated 'gate', *pylon*, is more often used for the gateway to a palace, temple, or private house than for the gate of a city (the usual word for which is *pyle*). Hence the gateway to the temple itself may be meant rather than a gate into the city.

Paul's speech is interesting because, unlike the other speeches we have heard so far, it is simply a call to worship the one true god and abandon idols (presumably this is what **follies** implies), and is not loaded with biblical quotations and allusions. The one direct quotation from the Septuagint, **who made heaven and earth and sea and everything in them** (v. 15; cf. Ex. 20.11) expresses an idea which would have been familiar at any rate to any of those present with a smattering of philosophy; the other claim for God, that **he sends you rain from heaven and crops in their seasons, and gives you food and good cheer in plenty** (v. 17) describes exactly what ordinary pagans wanted from their gods. This is a speech designed for Gentiles, rather than Jews or 'god-fearers'.

We now learn for the first time that Paul and Barnabas are being pursued by a posse of **Jews from Antioch and Iconium** (v. 19). The implication is that there were no Jews resident in Lystra; there has been no reference to a synagogue, and the people involved in the events narrated so far must have been pagans (without even such knowledge as a 'god-fearing' Gentile would have). There is no other evidence of Jewish settlement at Derbe or Lystra, except that Timothy who came from one of the two cities was the son of a Jewish mother (see 16.1; but Timothy had not been circumcised and so cannot have been brought up as a Jew), and *Acts* mentions 'Jews who lived in those parts' (16.3) with apparent reference to Lystra as well as Iconium. The absence of well-informed Gentiles would make these two places untypical of the cities Paul chose to evangelise, but he and Barnabas had been driven in flight to Lystra (and were to be driven on to Derbe) instead of choosing them for themselves; no doubt they made use of what opportunities they had.

The mood abruptly changes, and **they stoned Paul** (v. 19), which would be another attempted lynching, as at Iconium, rather than official action by the authorities. Paul is saved by **the converts** (v. 20), a group we have not met before. The narrative does not seem to allow an opportunity for serious converts yet to have been made at Lystra. The Greek word used, *mathetai*, also means 'disciples'. Were Paul and Barnabas perhaps accompanied by a group of followers? On the other hand, there are Christians at Lystra in 16.2.

They go next to Derbe, and then return to Lystra (now apparently quite safe again), Iconium, and Antioch, encouraging their converts, and establishing organised communities by appointing **elders for them in each congregation** (v. 23); the same word is used at 11.30 to refer to the leaders of the Jerusalem church.

From Pisidian Antioch they then return to their starting point, Syrian Antioch. There was a much more direct route overland from Derbe to Syria, through the Cilician Gates and Tarsus. The motive for retracing their steps was evidently to complete their mission in each of the cities from which they had been driven by violence by establishing the Christian community there on a firm basis.

Chapter 15

The conversion of Gentiles is challenged; Paul and Barnabas go to Jerusalem, and receive a ruling on the conditions under which Gentiles may be accepted into the church; Paul begins his travels again.

Up to this point, the admission of Gentiles to the church has continued without controversy, apart from some mild qualms initially (11.3) which are soon settled by Peter (11.18). Now, however, the status of Gentile Christians is called into question by **certain persons who had come down from Judaea** (v. 1). What they are reported as demanding of converts is circumcision, but no doubt the whole Mosaic law relating to purity and diet is implied. Paul uses the words 'foreskin' and 'circumcision' as labels for Gentiles and Jews (Gal. 2.7), and it may be that this is what is happening here. Certainly it would be the dietary and purity laws, rather than circumcision, which would be a barrier to social contact between Jewish and Gentile converts (and in any case circumcision would not apply to female converts). The judgement given later in this chapter is mostly about dietary rules. When Paul and Barnabas, and some others from the Antioch community, reach Jerusalem, the position of their opponents explicitly includes the demand that Gentiles should **keep the Law of Moses** (v. 5) as well as undergo circumcision. The proponents of this view are **some of the Pharisaic party** (v. 5; for religious parties, and Pharisees in particular see 5.17 and 5.34); it is not surprising to find Pharisees, members of the party devoted to the strictest interpretation of the Law, taking a similarly rigorous line after they had become Christians.

At a meeting of **apostles and elders** (v. 6) Peter speaks against the rigorists' view (vv. 7-11); Paul and Barnabas report on the success of their mission, and the signs (signifying God's approval) which have accompanied it (v. 12); James (the brother of Jesus, not the son of Zebedee, whose execution is reported at 12.2), supports Peter (vv. 13-21), and proposes a compromise, which is incorporated in a letter to be sent to Antioch with Paul and Barnabas and two of the Jerusalem community, **Judas and Silas** (v. 27). The actual text of the letter, like that of Lysias' letter in 23.26-30, was certainly composed by the author of *Acts* (see Introduction p. 30). Silas, like Paul, was a Roman citizen (16.37) and is referred to in Paul's epistles by a Latin 'family name' (*cognomen*) Silvanus (1 Thess. 1.1; 2 Thess. 1.1; 1 Cor. 2.19). Greek 'Silas' apparently represents a Semitic name meaning 'little wolf'. He may have chosen the common Latin name Silvanus ('woodsman') because of the similarity of sound with his Jewish name (see Introduction p. 26).

The decision of the meeting is not to require of Gentile converts circumcision and the full range of Jewish purity and dietary laws, but only **these essentials: you are to abstain from meat that has been offered to idols, from blood, from anything that has been strangled, and from fornication** (vv. 28-9). This is a curious list, and that it was found so in antiquity is shown by the additions to and subtractions from it (and its counterpart in James' speech at v. 20) found in the manuscript tradition. Some, perhaps embarrassed by the lack of any moral injunction, add: 'and to refrain from doing to others what they would not like done to themselves'. Others, no doubt finding the prohibition of fornication out of place in a list which is otherwise confined to matters of diet, omit it. Some manuscripts leave out the prohibition of things strangled.

Paul himself also discussed the problem of food offered to idols (see 1 Cor. ch. 8ff.). In pagan religion, a sacrifice was a meal shared with the god. Gods, like men, liked only certain parts of animals; fortunately, in most cases the parts which the gods required to be burnt on the altar at a sacrifice are just those parts which men do not like – the entrails and the bones; the remainder (the meat) was consumed by the worshippers. In the case of a large public sacrifice, the meat might be disposed of by being sold in the market. Invitations to social meals would often take the form of an invitation to participate in a sacrifice. So in order to avoid meat sacrificed to idols, it was not enough for a Christian simply to avoid taking part in pagan rituals (which would in any case surely be an uncontroversial requirement of converts, one which could be taken for granted). Paul himself seems to take the view that although eating meat sacrificed to idols is harmless in itself, because idols have no power (1 Cor. 8.4), nevertheless it is right to avoid it for the sake of the weaker brethren (1 Cor. 8.9-13). The ancients in general ate meat less often than is common today, and much of it may well have been consumed at festivals or social occasions, where there was a real prospect that some sort of offering to a god was involved (see Pliny, *Epistles* 10, 96, 10 and Williams' note, p. 143).

The prohibition of consuming blood is also part of the Mosaic Law (e.g. Lev. 17.10-14), and from it comes the ban on eating that which has been strangled, since the blood remains in an animal which has been slaughtered by strangling. Some, however, interpret blood as bloodshed; the Greek word *pniktos*, translated here 'strangled', is also a culinary term (e.g. Athenaeus 4, 147d), so some interpret this as a ban on gourmet food; if these interpretations were to be accepted, then taken with the prohibition on fornication we have three moral injunctions rather than dietary rules. Fornication, however, in itself is an odd vice to pick out for inclusion in this list of prohibitions. Both Jewish and Gentile moralists were against fornication, and it is impossible to make any assessment of whether actual practice differed very much in the two communities; it is a mistake to draw inferences about the behaviour of any group simply from the pronouncements of their more articulate moralists. The Jews, however, did prohibit sexual relations with a wider range of relatives than was normal among Gentiles (see Lev. 18.6-18), so that it may be that fornication really signifies irregular sexual intercourse. Paul seems to have met this problem in Corinth (1 Cor. 5.1-2). Alternatively, it may be used of worshipping false gods (compare *Hosea* ch. 4). In that case it would fit well with the dietary prohibitions.

Later, Jewish scholars formulated what they called 'the laws of Noah', that is to say, those laws of God which, unlike the laws of Moses, are laid upon all men, not just the Jews (see Schürer[2] III [1] pp. 171-3). It may be that this is a list of the same kind. Or, if we interpret the rules as essentially laws relating to diet and purity, it may represent what was necessary before Christians who still felt themselves bound by the law of Moses could feel that they could mix with Gentile Christians (for a discussion of the issues, see S.G. Wilson, *Luke and the Law*, pp. 68-102).

It is strange that this ruling should be referred to so little in later Christian writers. Paul never mentions it once, although he does deal with problems which seem to have been settled by this decision. *Revelation* (2.14) mentions eating food sacrificed to idols and fornication together, but there is no reason to believe that there is any reference to this decree; they go together in several biblical passages (e.g. Num. 25.1-2). Abstaining from blood is mentioned by Tertullian (*Apol.* 9, 13-14), who claims that pagans used to test Christians by trying to tempt them into eating black pudding (*botulos...cruore distentos*), and by Minucius Felix (30, 6). It also occurs in a report given by Eusebius (*Ecclesiastical History* 5, 1, 26) of an incident during the martyrdoms at Lyon in 177, when a woman called Biblis, who had denied that she was a Christian, was put to torture to get her to give evidence of Christian cannibalism, and cried out: 'How would such men eat children, when they are not allowed to eat the blood even of irrational animals?' In all three passages the prohibition of blood is mentioned in the context of an argument refuting charges that Christians indulged in cannibalism; all of them were written at a time when the source of knowledge of the decree might be *Acts* itself, rather than an independent tradition.

Another problem is the relationship of this meeting to the one related by Paul in *Galatians* chapter 2. Though they are on the same subject (the status of Gentile converts), Paul makes no mention in *Galatians* of any set of rulings such as we have here, and the role of Peter and James (and indeed Barnabas) is quite different. If both are reports of the same meeting, someone is misleading us. On the other hand, if they are different meetings (and Paul in *Galatians* mentions only two visits to Jerusalem at the time that the letter was written) then the second visit of *Galatians* should be the one mentioned at *Acts* 11.30 and 12.25, of which we are told virtually nothing. This would mean that the letter to the Galatians was written, before the meeting of chapter 15, to the four cities of Phrygia and Lycaonia which he has just visited, which are in the province, but not the region, of Galatia. For a discussion of the question of the recipients of *Galatians*, see note on 16.6.

After returning to Antioch, Paul and Barnabas decide to revisit the communities they have founded. Unusually in *Acts*, we have now a record of a real quarrel. It appears that the departure of John Mark at 13.13 had caused some ill-feeling. **Barnabas wanted to take John Mark with them** (v. 37), but Paul took the view that he **had deserted them in Pamphylia** (v. 38), and will not travel with him. They part, Barnabas and John Mark going to Cyprus, while Paul, taking Silas with him, travels **through Syria and Cilicia** (v. 41), using this time the direct route overland from Antioch to Galatia (see note on 14.21). It may be that this episode had some significance to the author's intended audience, but there is no way of knowing what it might have been.

Chapter 16

After travelling through Asia Minor to the coast, they are instructed in a dream to cross to Macedonia; at Philippi they expel a spirit from a girl; Paul and Silas are arrested, flogged, and imprisoned; next morning they reveal that they are Roman citizens, and are released with an apology.

After Paul travels on **to Derbe and to Lystra** (v. 1: see notes on 14.6 and 19; on the route north-west from Tarsus they would reach Derbe before

Lystra), he finds **there…a disciple named Timothy, the son of a Jewish Christian mother and a Gentile** (or more literally, with *RSV*, **Greek**) **father** (v. 1). It is not clear whether 'there' means Lystra or Derbe. The Greek word translated here as 'there', *ekei*, is used in the classical period to refer to the more distant of two places or to the former of two names (the nearer of two places and the latter of two names would be referred to by using *enthade* or *autou*, 'here'); according to this usage *ekei* should refer to Derbe. But, as Bruce comments (p. 351), Lystra is 'the common term between "Derbe and Lystra" (v. 1) and "Lystra and Iconium" (v. 2)'. However, it could be argued that the brethren of Lystra and Iconium are mentioned as speaking well of Timothy (v. 2) just because neither city was his native place. His name, presumably chosen by his father, is a purely Greek one, and indeed one used in classical Athens (e.g. the great general of the 4th century BC). The two elements allude to honour (*time*) and to 'god' (*theos*), but since no specific pagan god is named it would not offend Jewish susceptibilities. Timothy is the addressee of two of the Pastoral Epistles (whose ascription to Paul is contested) and is referred to in several of Paul's epistles (1 Thess. 1.1, 3.2 and 6; Phil. 1.1, 2.19 and 23; 1 Cor. 4.17, 16.10; 2 Cor. 1.1 and 19; Col. 1.1; Phlm. 1). It is interesting that the word 'Greek' (*Hellen*) is used here and in v. 3 almost as a synonym for Gentile.

Wishing to have Timothy as a companion, he **circumcised him, out of consideration for the Jews who lived in those parts** (v. 3), one of the actions ascribed to Paul in *Acts* whose historical authenticity has been most fiercely attacked because of its inconsistency with the principles of the author of the Epistles (see Introduction p. 9).

NEB's **they travelled through the Phrygian and Galatian region** (v. 6), does not really convey the ambiguity of the Greek, which is neatly conveyed by the *RSV*'s **they went through the region of Phrygia and Galatia.** Does it refer to a single geographical area or two distinct ones? The Greek has been interpreted as meaning (a) Phrygia and the Galatian country, or (b) the country that is both Phrygian and Galatian. The Greek word *Phrygian* could be either the proper name Phrygia or the adjective 'Phrygian' (the claim made by Kirsopp Lake in BC V, p. 231, that the feminine form of the adjective was not used in post-classical Greek, was demolished by the citation of numerous examples by C.J. Hemer in *J. Theol. Stud.* 27, pp. 122-6 and 28, pp. 99-101). The second part of the phrase can only mean 'Galatian country'.

If (a) is correct, then Paul travelled through part of Phrygia, and *then* through an area which could be described as 'Galatian'. Since he was revisiting the churches founded on his previous journey, he presumably visited Antioch as well as Iconium, both of which in fact lay in the region where the Phrygian language was spoken (see notes on 13.14 and 14.1).

The 'Galatian country' would lie on their route north from Iconium or Antioch towards the province of Bithynia (see v. 7) and it has been widely assumed that the phrase referred to the region in the north of the Anatolian plateau which had been occupied by three Celtic-speaking tribes in the 3rd century BC. These people were called *Galatai*, 'Gauls', in Greek, and their new country Galatia. But the direct route north from the area of Antioch and Iconium toward Bithynia passed through an area which was Phrygian in language and culture (W.M. Calder, *Monumenta Asiae Minoris Antiqua*, vol. 7, pp. xii-xiii, n. 6). In fact, many of the older maps of Paul's journeys mark a diversion a long way to the north-east and east as far as Ankyra or even Tavium, the heartland of the Galatians, because it was assumed, from the 4th to the 18th centuries, that the recipients of Paul's epistle *To the Galatians* were churches in the country of the Gauls (and also rightly held that such churches ought to have been in the main towns of the region).

If (b) is correct, it could either mean an area where both the Phrygian and the Galatian languages were spoken (Lake, BC V, 236) or that part of Phrygia which lay inside the Roman province of Galatia (i.e. the region of Iconium and Antioch). The latter was the hypothesis of W.M. Ramsay (*The Church in the Roman Empire*, 5th edn, pp. 75-89 and 484-8), who argued that in this Greek phrase the author was echoing a piece of Roman official nomenclature, the Latin phrase *Phrygia Galatica*, 'Galatian Phrygia'. Although there are no actual records of this phrase being used, there are epigraphic examples of analogous ones: *Pontus Galaticus* referring to that part of Pontus incorporated in the province was distinguished from *Pontus Polemonianus*, the part assigned to the client king Polemon (Dessau no. 1017, translated in Introduction p. 23); *Lycaonia Antiochiana* was applied to that part of Lycaonia handed over to Antiochus IV (see note on 14.6; Dessau no. 1364) presumably to distinguish it from the part which remained in the province of Galatia. (Ramsay's hypothesis is defended by Bruce, *Bull. John Ryl. Lib.*, vol. 52, 255-9; cf. *Paul, Apostle of the Free Spirit*, p. 166).

The interpretation of this phrase in v. 6 has aroused fierce controversy as part of a wider debate about the identity of the 'Galatians' to whom Paul's epistle was addressed. The commentators of the patristic age took it for granted that they were 'Galatians' in the sense of *Galatai* because the Roman province of Galatia had by the 4th century AD been reduced to the original territory of the Galatians. Not until the mid-18th century was it proposed that the recipients of the epistle were the four churches in the *province* of Galatia (as it existed in Paul's day), the founding of which was described in *Acts* 13-14 (viz. Antioch, Iconium, Lystra, and Derbe). This application of Occam's Razor (why conjure up out of this verse of *Acts* a mission to Ankyra when four 'Galatian' foundations are well attested?) has continued to be opposed by many biblical scholars. But how could Paul have addressed the Christians in these four cities collectively except as Galatians? On the other hand, when he calls them 'You stupid Galatians!' (Gal. 3.1) Paul seems to be laying quite an unnecessary emphasis on the term 'Galatian'. Is it possible that Paul here is gently teasing the recipients of his letter by reminding them that they lived in a province which took its name from a region not noted for its sophistication or culture, and that in their foolishness they ran the risk, not just of being called, but also of behaving like Galatians? (The authors owe this suggestion to Professor Fergus Millar).

Paul's intention must have been to travel westwards from Iconium and Antioch, across the boundary between the provinces of Galatia and Asia, and to head for the prosperous cities on the east coast of the Aegean, such as Ephesus (19.1), with their flourishing Jewish communities and attendant 'god-fearers' (see Introduction p. 21; Schürer[2] III [1] pp. 17-26). He is, however, **prevented by the Holy Spirit from delivering the message in the province of Asia** (v. 6), though we are not told by what means the spirit delivered its message.

Next, **when they approached the Mysian border, they tried to enter Bithynia** (v. 7), presumably intending to make for the great cities of Nicomedia and Nicaea in the heart of Bithynia proper (the western half of the province of *Bithynia et Pontus*): for evidence of Jewish settlement see Schürer[2] III (1) pp. 35-6. (In contrast, 'for Galatia proper the evidence is very sparse' Schürer[2] III [1] p. 34; nor does *Acts* give any indication of a plan to push east to Ankyra and Tavium: see note on v. 6). The routes north from Iconium or Antioch would run through Phrygian country on either side of the provincial boundary between Galatia and Asia. A point on this route short of the actual boundary of Bithynia but 'in the latitude of Mysia' would lie in the region of Prymnesos (Calder, *Monumenta Asiae Minoris Antiqua* 7, loc. cit.). Again, however, **the Spirit of Jesus would not allow them** (v. 7); there is no indication of whether the 'Spirit of Jesus' signifies anything different from 'the Holy Spirit', nor of how the instruction was communicated. The important point, however, is that again we see Paul's mission to the Gentiles being guided by God, which guarantees that God approves of it. The same point is made in v. 9 when a vision is given to Paul to guide him to the next stage of his journey.

They skirted Mysia and reached the coast at Troas (v. 8); Mysia was a mountainous, forested area in the north-west corner of Asia Minor, difficult to cross by road. Travellers going from a point south of the boundary of Bithynia to Troas on the Aegean coast west of Mysia would probably have skirted the main mountainous area on its southern side. Alexandria Troas (to be distinguished from Ilium farther north, which was regarded at the time as the successor of Homer's Troy) was created by the fusion of smaller Greek cities in the area under Alexander the Great's successors (and named after him); a Roman citizen colony had been planted there under Augustus (C.J. Hemer, *Tyndale Bulletin* 26, pp. 79-112). W.P. Bowers (*J. Theol. Stud.* [1979] pp. 509-11) rightly points out that no-one would have taken this route and chosen Troas as a port unless he was wanting to travel by sea in a north-westerly direction (i.e. to Thrace or Macedonia).

A vision of a Macedonian comes to Paul at night, as a result of which **we at once set about getting a passage to Macedonia** (v. 10). This is the first appearance of the mysterious 'we' in *Acts* (see Introduction p. 12). Macedonia refers to the Roman province of that name which extended across the Balkan peninsula from a point midway along the north coast of the Aegean to the Adriatic, and so included much territory in addition to the original homeland of the *Makedones*, the people of Philip and Alexander.

Ancient vessels (apart from warships) were usually wholly dependent on the wind, so when the author tells us that **we sailed from Troas and made a straight run to Samothrace, the next day to Neapolis** (v. 11), he must mean that they had a favourable wind; in contrast it took Paul five days to make the reverse crossing at a later date (20.6; BC IV, p. 186 and Bruce, p. 356). The stop at the island of Samothrace may reflect the preference of ancient merchant ships for sticking to coastlines or hopping between islands, or their practice of collecting and disposing of small items of cargo at numerous ports on their routes (cf. F. Braudel, *The Mediterranean*, vol. I, p. 107 for a description of such 'tramping' in the 16th century Mediterranean; he likens the ships to 'small travelling bazaars'; see pp. 103-8 for the practice of 'coastal navigation'; cf. note on 21.3). Neapolis was the most easterly port on the Aegean coast of the province of Macedonia, and the obvious destination after the decision taken at Troas.

They first make for **Philippi, a city of the first rank in that district of Macedonia, and a Roman colony** (v. 12). The Greek city of Philippi had been founded (and named after himself) by Philip II of Macedon in an area of gold and silver mines which he had seized. A Roman citizen colony was probably first planted there after the victory of the Caesarian army over Julius Caesar's assassin, Marcus Brutus, nearby in 42 BC. Its Latin name was *Colonia Iulia Augusta Philippensis*.

The Greek phrase which is translated 'a city of the first rank in that district of Macedonia' by *NEB*, and 'the leading city of the district of Macedonia' by *RSV*, does not appear in that form in all of the manuscripts, and presents some problems. Most of the Greek manuscripts have the adjective 'first' linked to 'city', and the noun 'district' linked to 'Macedonia', with or without definite articles; the 'Western' text alone reads '*head* of Macedonia'. It is the use of the Greek word *meris* (translated 'district') in connection with Macedonia which has led to a proposal to emend the text to read 'a city of (in) the first district of Macedonia'. This Greek term is an inappropriate one to apply to Macedonia as a whole, whether to the original kingdom or to the (larger) Roman province (and indeed Macedonia has twice been mentioned without any such description: vv. 9-10). On the other hand, it is known that the portion of the Roman province which had formed the territory of the old kingdom was subdivided into four districts, and the Greek term used for such a district was *meris*. When the Romans deposed the last king, Perseus, in 168 BC, they experimented with a division of his kingdom into four self-governing republics; these were incorporated in a permanent province after a rebellion twenty years later, but the evidence of inscriptions and coins shows that these four *merides* continued to have a corporate existence under the Roman governors, with their own councils (*synedria*), down at least to the 1st century. These four 'districts' had no proper names but were simply called 1st, 2nd, 3rd, 4th. It is known that Philippi lay within the boundaries of the First *Meris* (Livy 45, 29, 5). The correction 'a city of the First *Meris* of Macedonia' is thus overwhelmingly convincing. (Some manuscripts of the Latin Vulgate and translations derived from them read 'of the first part', but this is probably the result of errors by their copyists, rather than of access to a Greek text with the correct reading.) The author of *Acts* had accurate knowledge of a unique feature of Macedonian administration (cf. note on 17.6), but those who copied his text did not, and 'corrected' the text to read 'first city of the *meris*' instead of 'a city of the First *Meris*'. (Sherwin-White [1963] pp. 93-5, suggested that the author wrote 'first city (i.e. a leading city) of the First District'; in Greek, two forms of the word 'first' would have stood next to each other, *prote tes protes*, so it would not be surprising if this was miscopied as simple *protes*. However, one would suppose that the author would have noticed, and avoided, such a confusing combination of words.)

On the Sabbath they go to a place **where we thought there would be a place of prayer** (v. 13). The Greek word *proseuche*, translated 'place of prayer', actually means simply 'prayer', but in a Jewish context it was frequently used for a congregation or the building in which it met, i.e. as the equivalent of 'synagogue' (Schürer[2] II, p. 425). Elsewhere in *Acts*, however, Jewish congregations are always referred to as 'synagogues', and it could be deduced from the end of this verse that only women were present, in which case no lawful synagogue service could be held (Bruce, p. 358; a minimum number of ten men, *minyan*, is required). It is not clear what sort of gathering the author is describing (Schürer[2] III (1) p. 65, supplies no evidence other than this passage for the existence of a synagogue at Philippi).

The one convert made as a result of the visits of Paul and his companions to the *proseuche* is **one of them named Lydia, a dealer in purple fabric from the city of Thyatira, who was a worshipper of God** (v. 14) (presumably, then, she was a Gentile 'god-fearer'). Lydia was used as a personal name, but its original meaning was 'Lydian woman'. Thyatira was a city in Lydia, which is probably why she came to be known as 'Lydia' in Philippi (though it is not impossible that she also had another personal name). Her native city had an association of dyers (*Inscr. Graec. ad res Rom. pert.* IV, nos 1213, 1250, 1265). Purple (*porphyra*) usually refers to the famous Tyrian purple obtained from the *murex* shellfish, but see Bruce p. 358 for a suggestion that in this case it may refer to a local Lydian vegetable dye. In any case, purple cloth was always a luxury item.

As a result of Paul's preaching Lydia **was baptised, and her household with her** (v. 15). The word translated 'household', *oikos*, like the Latin *familia*, covers not only kindred but also slaves, of whom Lydia probably owned a number who worked in her dyeing business (free men serving full-time as hired employees were rare in the ancient economy: see M.I. Finley, *The Ancient Economy*, ch. 3). One wonders how much choice the slaves had about baptism. This passage, and others in *Acts* recording the baptism of entire households, have frequently been used in disputes over the rightness of infant baptism (since a large *oikos* would very likely include small children).

The next encounter of Paul and Silas is with **a slave girl who was possessed by an oracular spirit and brought large profits to her owners by telling fortunes** (v. 16). The Greek phrase behind 'oracular spirit' is *pneuma Pythona*. Plutarch (*De Defectu Oraculorum* 414E) reports that soothsayers were called 'pythons' in allusion to *the* Python, the serpent killed by Apollo which originally occupied the oracle at Delphi; for *pneuma* see note on 1.2. The mention of 'owners' in the plural suggests that a slave could be owned by more than one person. The slave-girl follows Paul and his companions **shouting 'These men are servants of the Supreme God'** (v. 17). In the Septuagint translation of the Hebrew bible the Greek phrase *theos hypsistos* (= 'the Most High God') is used when non-Israelites speak of the God of Israel, and Josephus has Augustus refer to 'the High Priest of the Most High God' (*Ant.* 16, 163). The author of *Acts* would have thought this an appropriate way for a Gentile to refer to the God of Israel. Whether he was also aware of the existence of cults of the Most High God by 'judaizing' Gentiles such as are attested in inscriptions (see BC V, pp. 90-6; A.D. Nock, *Essays on Religion and the Ancient World* I, pp. 414-43) is of course unknown to us. Finally, in exasperation, Paul drives the spirit from the girl, as a result of which her owners, having lost a good source of income, **seized Paul and Silas and dragged them to the city authorities in the main square** (v. 19). The translation 'main square' (like *RSV*'s 'market place') is a little misleading. The Greek word translated is *agora*, whose root is the same as that of the verb *agoreuein*, 'to deliver a speech'. In the Homeric poems it refers to the place the people assembled for debate. The word is used to translate the Latin *forum*, and since Philippi was a Roman colony the open space referred to here was a *forum*; every colony was provided with a square which was surrounded by the main public buildings and was the seat of the courts and the elected officials. 'Authorities' represents the Greek *archontes*, the general term for the chief officials of each city (see Introduction p. 17). In this case they are identical with the **magistrates** of v. 20; the Greek word used in that verse is *strategoi* which originally meant 'generals' (literally = 'army-leaders'), but by the 1st century it was widely used of officials with purely civilian functions. It was also used as the Greek equivalent of the Latin *praetores*, the second highest ranking magistrates at Rome itself. The suggestion of Bruce (p. 362) that the senior magistrates of Philippi were called *praetores* as a courtesy title and that it was for that reason that *strategoi* is used in this verse must be rejected. As in all colonies outside Italy, the pair of senior magistrates at Philippi were called *duoviri iure dicundo* (literally = 'two men for saying law'); Sherwin-White (1963, pp. 92-3) is right to say that a colourless Greek word is being used to render an untranslatable Latin title.

The charge is: **'These men are causing a disturbance in our city; they are Jews; they are advocating customs which it is illegal for us Romans to adopt and follow'** (vv. 20-1). Sherwin-White (1963, pp. 78-9) points out that correct legal procedure is being followed. In a society without police or state prosecutors it was up to private persons to bring criminal charges before the appropriate authorities, and at Philippi the *duoviri* were the chief judges. Of the two charges, 'provoking a riot/disturbing the peace' is straightforward, but the second one, inducing the colonists to adopt 'un-Roman' practices is puzzling. The stress on the fact that the accused are Jews, in addition to arousing anti-Jewish prejudice, (for which see Schürer[2] III [1] pp. 150-3), is surely intended to indicate that the 'customs' are worship of the god of the Jews and adherence to Jewish law. The stress on 'it is illegal for us Romans' (i.e. the plaintiffs as citizens of Philippi as well as the *duoviri*) appeals to the sense of superiority felt by the people of Philippi, Romans isolated in a sea of Greeks, over 'lesser breeds', but whether it was in fact 'illegal' ('not allowed' is a more precise translation) for Romans to participate in foreign cults at this date is debatable. Theodor Mommsen developed the theory that there was a basic principle of Roman law that Romans were not allowed to take part in the cult of any foreign gods which had not been approved by the Senate. At an earlier period, when the Roman citizen body had been much smaller, more cohesive, and wholly Italian, there may well have been a strong prejudice of this kind, but there had been no consistent efforts to enforce it in recent centuries (and the extension of citizenship to people from a wide range of cultures would have made it impractical; see Sherwin-White [1963] pp. 78-9, and Appendix 5 to his *Letters of Pliny*). In any case prosecutors in Roman courts would throw in any complaints which they thought would prejudice the judges against the defendants, regardless of the precise state of the law.

The mob joined in the attack (v. 22) or, more literally, 'rose up together against them'. Since the magistrates proceeded to inflict formal punishment, the 'attack' must imply not physical assault and riot, but shouts and gestures of hostility. The magistrates **ordered them to be flogged** (v. 22; translated more literally by *RSV* **gave orders to beat them with rods**). The *duoviri* would be escorted by lictors (see v. 35) carrying the *fasces* (bundles of rods), the symbol of their right to inflict corporal punishment. Such beatings are described by Sherwin-White (1963) as 'cautionary' (pp. 27-8, 75-6), inflicted along with a stern warning. They were held to be appropriate for those who started fires through negligence or for the ancient equivalent of 'soccer hooligans' (*Digest* 1, 15, 3, 1; 48, 19, 28, 3). A passage from the early 3rd century jurist Paulus is apposite to the case of Paul and Silas: 'soothsayers who pretend to be inspired by a god should be expelled from a city...after first being beaten with rods, they are expelled from the city' (*Sententiae Pauli* 5, 21, 1). When they are **flung...into prison** (v. 23), however, it is not as part of their punishment. Imprisonment in a town gaol was not used as a penalty in Roman law; the equivalent to long terms of imprisonment inflicted in modern states was a sentence of forced labour or work in the mines. Detention in town gaols was the equivalent of modern detention 'on remand' to await trial. In this case such 'remand' could only be to await trial by the proconsul of Macedonia on his assize circuit (see note on 19.38). There is no certainty about the limitations on the criminal jurisdiction of local magistrates or about which matters were reserved for the provincial governors (Sherwin-White [1963] pp. 74-6; P. Garnsey, *JRS* [1968] p. 53). On the other hand, the intention may just have been to detain them overnight before a formal expulsion of the kind referred to by the jurist Paulus (see note on v. 22; cf. vv. 35-6, 39). **The jailer** (v. 23) to whom they are entrusted would probably be a 'public slave', owned by the colony of Philippi; most 'local government officers' in ancient cities were slaves (see Pliny, *Epistles* 10, 19, 1, with notes by Sherwin-White and Williams). The jailer **secured their feet in the stocks** (v. 24), or, more literally, 'the wood'. Regulations for local city jurisdiction at Pergamum in Asia laid down that slaves who misused public fountains should be fastened 'in the wood' for ten days (OGIS II, no. 483, 1. 181); and accounts of the later punishment of Christians depict it as an instrument of torture (Eusebius, *Ecclesiastical History* 5, 1, 27; 6, 39, 5).

During the night, an earthquake bursts open the doors and frees the prisoners from their fetters. The jailer, assuming the prisoners had escaped, **drew his sword intending to kill himself** (v. 27). Suggestions that this might be 'as a point of military honour' (BC IV, p. 198) are based on a misconception about the jailer's status. Paul reassures him, and as a result **he and his whole family were baptised** (v. 33). Presumably his family is the same as his **household** (v. 31), i.e. his *oikos* (see note on v. 15). Though a slave himself, his *oikos* might well include slaves; under Roman law slaves might be permitted by their owners to amass property which they could treat as their own (*peculium*), and this often included slaves.

When daylight came the magistrates sent their officers with instructions to release the men (v. 35), but neither here nor in the narrative which follows do they show any awareness of the earthquake. The miracle story has not been neatly dovetailed into the main narrative. This troubled the editor of the 'Western' text, who inserted two long passages in vv. 35 and 38 reporting reactions to the earthquake, and so masking the gap. The officers sent are, in Greek, *rhabdouchoi* (literally = 'rod-holders'), and this was the usual word used to translate the Latin *lictores*, the title of a peculiarly Roman group of officers. At Rome the consuls and praetors were attended in public by men carrying bundles of rods (*fasces*) which symbolised their power as magistrates. Since each citizen colony was a miniature copy of Rome, the *duoviri* in each (the local equivalent of the consuls) would have their own lictors, who would be sent to transmit their official orders. The closest English equivalent would be 'beadles'. The author of *Acts* has accurate information about Philippi; in ordinary provincial cities there would not be any lictors.

When the lictors arrive at the gaol, Paul makes a complaint: **They gave us a public flogging, though we are Roman citizens, and have not been found guilty** (v. 37). 'Public' is an ambiguous translation. The Greek adverb *demosiai* does not mean 'in full view of the public', but 'officially', 'as a public act of the state'. The claim that they had not been found guilty is also a surprise; one would expect a complaint that they had not had a trial, i.e. that they had had no opportunity to offer a defence (and there is no hint in v. 22 that they were allowed to do so); and this would be a much more serious charge than that the *duoviri* had omitted to deliver a formal sentence before ordering them to be beaten. The literal meaning of the Greek word is 'without being condemned', but the author of *Acts* may have intended it to imply 'without a proper trial' (cf. BC IV, p. 200). This is the first time that the fact that Paul and Silas were Roman citizens is stated in *Acts*, no doubt because this is the first occasion when the reader needs to know it to understand what follows. Why Paul had not revealed it earlier at Philippi is not explained; Haenchen's suggestion (p. 504) that Paul wanted to avoid long delays resulting from a formal appeal is less plausible than the hypothesis that the violent scene described in v. 22 did not really allow any chance for them to exploit their status.

The magistrates were alarmed to hear that they were Roman

citizens, and came and apologised to them (v. 38). Since the *duoviri* were the elected chief magistrates of a Roman colony, they exercised jurisdiction over Roman citizens as part of their official functions. Is the author being accurate in representing them as being so alarmed? He probably is, both on technical, legal grounds, and in broader terms of the 'clout' a Roman citizen carried. It is probable that a flogging should not have been inflicted on Roman citizens without their being allowed an opportunity to appeal (the precise legal rights of citizens at this date are discussed in the note to 25.11-12). In any case, it was still felt to be improper or unwise in the middle of the 1st century for municipal magistrates in the provinces (even in Roman colonies) to treat Roman citizens in the rough and ready way in which this pair of *duoviri* thought they could get away with treating itinerant Jewish religious enthusiasts. In the provinces Roman citizens were still a small minority and regarded as members of the ruling people, entitled to different treatment from the subject peoples, whatever their social status might be. The picture given in *Acts* actually represents the situation at the time of the events it narrates. A hundred years later the special standing enjoyed by Roman citizens had been eroded, except in the case of those of high rank; in the 180s tenant farmers in imperial estates in North Africa complained to the emperor Commodus that an imperial official 'had ordered some, even Roman citizens, to be beaten with rods and cudgels' (Dessau no. 6870 col. 2. ll. 13-14). See Sherwin-White (1963) pp. 172-4, and P. Garnsey, *Social Status and Legal Privilege in the Roman Empire.*

Though the magistrates apologise, they nevertheless **requested them to go away from the city** (v. 39).

Chapter 17

Paul and Silas are driven from Thessalonica and Beroea; at Athens Paul gives an address at the Areopagus.

They now travelled by way of Amphipolis and Apollonia and came to Thessalonica, where there was a Jewish synagogue (v. 1), travelling west along the main Roman highway across the Balkan peninsula which ran from the Straits of Otranto to the Bosporus, the Via Egnatia. Thessalonica was founded in the late 4th century BC by Cassander the ruler of Macedon on the site of an older Greek city, Therme, at the head of the gulf of the same name, and named after Cassander's wife, the half-sister of Alexander the Great. It eventually became (and still remains) the most populous town in Macedonia and northern Greece. After taking the Caesarian side in the civil war of 42 BC it was rewarded with the status of 'free city' (see Introduction pp. 16-17). Reference books and commentaries refer to it as 'the seat of administration' (Bruce p. 369) or 'residence of the proconsul' (Haenchen p. 506), yet the proconsuls of Macedonia must have been peripatetic, without any permanent residence, just like those of Asia and other provinces (see Introduction p. 25). Furthermore, if the same rules applied to Thessalonica as applied at Aphrodisias, the proconsul should not even have visited the city without the emperor's permission (J. Reynolds, *Aphrodisias and Rome*, pp. 120-4, 175-6). For evidence of Jews at Thessalonica, and for the existence of a Samaritan community, see Schürer² III (1) 66-7.

In Thessalonica **following his usual practice Paul went to their meetings** (sc. of the synagogue) **and for the next three Sabbaths he argued with them** (v. 2). For Paul's practice see Introduction pp. 9-10, and notes on 13.15-16; his converts here seem to have included Jews as well as Gentile 'god-fearers' (v. 4). If he appeared at the synagogue on 'three Sabbaths', then he was there for a period of between two and three weeks (see BC IV, 202-3). The implication that Paul was driven out after his first fortnight is in contradiction to what he says in 1 *Thessalonians* 2.9 and *Philippians* 4.16, both of which suggest a longer visit during which Paul worked to support himself, and the Christians of Philippi several times sent him aid (Haenchen 510f.).

The trouble which breaks out after this promising start is attributed by the author to **the Jews in their jealousy** (v. 5), presumably arising from their fear of losing financial support from the **godfearing Gentiles** (v. 4). An inscription from Aphrodisias shows such men providing help for the synagogue there (Reynolds and Tannenbaum, *Jews and Godfearers*, p. 5 ll. 19-20); compare also Cornelius 'who gave generously to help the Jewish people' (10.2). The Jews then **recruited some low fellows from the dregs of the populace, roused the rabble, and had the city in an uproar** (v. 5). The phrase 'roused the rabble' translates a single word in Greek which literally means 'made a mob'; the 'dregs of society' translates the Greek *agoraioi* (literally = the men of the market-place), i.e. the sort of people who hang around in public waiting for something to happen. On urban violence see Introduction pp. 18-20. **They mobbed Jason's house, with the intention of bringing Paul and Silas before the town assembly** (v. 5). Jason, whom we have not met before, is presumably one of the converts; Jason is a perfectly normal Greek name, but he could be a Jew, since at least one High Priest called Joshua went by the name of Jason in Greek, presumably as the nearest equivalent (2 Macc. 4.7). 'Town assembly' translates the Greek word *demos*, which can refer both to 'the masses' and to the citizen body of a Greek *polis* which constituted its ultimate political and judicial authority. Ramsay (*St Paul*, p. 228), Bruce (p. 370), and Sherwin-White (1963, pp. 96 and 175) held that it was used in the latter sense here, and that a formal prosecution before the Assembly of citizens (whose decisions would be immune to interference by the proconsul, since Thessalonica was a 'free city') was envisaged. However, Lake and Cadbury rightly point out that the context requires *demos* to be taken in the former sense; the word is used as a synonym for *ochlos* (crowd, mob) in the verb 'making a mob (= *ochlos*)' earlier (BC IV, p. 205; see notes on 19.30-5). What was planned, presumably, was some ancient equivalent of 'tarring and feathering' and 'riding out of town on a rail' (Mark Twain, *Huckleberry Finn* ch. 19).

They fail to find Paul and Silas, so instead **they dragged Jason himself and some members of the congregation before the magistrates** (v. 6), before, that is, the *politarchai*, a college of elected officers who formed the chief executive of the city (like the *duoviri* of Philippi). The use of this title (instead of the general term *archontes*) shows once again (cf. 16.12) that the author is well informed about local administration in Macedonia. The title *politarches* occurs nowhere else in Greek literature, but it does appear on inscriptions from several cities in Macedonia, and only in Macedonia. Jason and his associates are formally charged before the appropriate authorities; perhaps their enemies did not dare to use against citizens of Thessalonica (some of them perhaps men of substance) the methods they had planned to use against Paul.

The accusation they bring is: **The men who have made trouble all over the world have now come here; and Jason has harboured them. They all flout the emperor's laws, and assert that there is a rival king, Jesus.** (vv. 6-7). This is a mixture of general prejudice ('made trouble all over the world'; perhaps an allusion to events at Philippi) and specific charges, viz. violating 'the emperor's laws' and proclaiming allegiance to another ruler than Claudius. The latter presumably was a distortion of some of Paul's teachings about Jesus and, if taken seriously, would certainly worry anyone in authority. Attempts have been made to identify particular pronouncements of Claudius which might be being referred to: for example, a letter of Claudius to the city of Alexandria in AD 41 (preserved on a papyrus: A.S. Hunt and C.C. Edgar, *Select Papyri* II, 212, l. 100) in which the emperor referred to Jews who were stirring up a universal plague (Sherwin-White [1963] p. 103; cf. note on 24.5). But an imperial letter to a city in one province would not be circulated in those of another. The allegation need not have been specific, but just another way of drumming up hostility.

The magistrates **bound over Jason and the others, and let them go** (v. 9). The phrase 'bound over' (more literally translated by *RSV* **taken security**) represents Greek words meaning 'taking the sufficient', and is a literal translation of a Latin legal phrase for requiring the provision of a financial guarantee to a court. This Latinism had come into common use in

Greek in the eastern provinces (Sherwin-White [1963] p. 95; BC IV, p. 206). The guarantee would be forfeited if the person involved failed to perform some obligation, e.g. to turn up for trial (but there is no suggestion of that in this case); presumably Jason had to promise not to harbour Paul and Silas, which explains why they leave under cover of night (v. 10).

Their next destination is **Beroea** (v. 10), a town in Macedonia, southwest from Thessalonica and inland. It was the city where the 'provincial council' of delegates from the cities of Macedonia met to conduct the ceremonies of the provincial cult of the emperor, so that if a 'capital' has to be identified for the province, Beroea is as good a candidate as any. As usual Paul first visits **the synagogue** (v. 10), where he is initially well received. The only other evidence for Jewish residents in Beroea is two epitaphs of the late-Roman period (Schürer[2] III [1] p. 67). When, however, trouble is stirred up by Jews from Thessalonica, the Christians there send Paul **off at once to go down to the coast** (v. 14), leaving Silas and Timothy behind. Paul is brought **as far as Athens** (v. 15), where he waits for his companions. The obvious deduction to make from this account is that Paul went to a port on the coast east of Beroea, and travelled by ship to Athens. The arguments of Lake and Cadbury (BC IV, pp. 207-8) that 'to the coast' refers to the same journey as 'as far as Athens', and that Paul actually travelled by land to Athens, are unconvincing. Had the author intended the reader to infer this, he was unusually clumsy and obscure. (And in fact the town of Athens itself is four miles from the sea.)

The account of Paul's activities while he **was waiting for them at Athens** (v. 16) has been the subject of lively controversy. On the one hand, some scholars (especially M. Dibelius, *Studies in Acts* chs 2-3; A.D. Nock, *Essays in Religion and the Ancient World* II, pp. 821-32; Haenchen, pp. 527-31) suggest that the account in *Acts* represents a symbolic confrontation between Paul and the Gentile world (the counterpart to his earlier encounters with the Jewish world), taking place in what is felt to be the intellectual and cultural heart of that world, Athens, and displaying little knowledge of the reality of the Athens Paul might have visited; in other words, it is a literary device with only a casual connection with what might have actually happened. Others (e.g. T.D. Barnes, 'An Apostle on Trial' *J. Theol. Stud.* vol. 20 (1969) pp. 407-19; C.J. Hemer, 'Paul at Athens' *New Test. Stud.* vol. 20, pp. 341-50) argue that the picture of Athens given is one which in a number of details tallies perfectly with what is known of Athens in the middle of the 1st century, and is not an idealised one derived from literary sources.

By the 1st century AD Athens was far from being the rich and populous city it had been at its height in the 5th and 4th centuries BC. In 88-87 BC it became involved in a war against Rome, and was besieged and taken by storm in 86 BC by the Roman general Sulla, who imposed on it a constitution in line with Rome's preference for upper-class rule; it did however have the status of a 'free and allied city' (see Introduction p. 17). The importance of Athens at this period was as a cultural centre. Its glorious past and famous monuments attracted many visitors and benefactions from emperors (see P. Graindor, *Athènes d'Auguste à Trajan*; D.W. Geagan in *ANRW* II [7.1] pp. 382-9). Its rhetorical and philosophical schools had for a long time attracted young men to spend brief periods there to 'finish their education'.

In philosophy, the attractions of Athens were twofold. First, Athens was the setting for the philosophical dialogues of Plato and Xenophon, which would probably be any young man's first encounter with philosophy, since they were widely read as models of good Greek style. These dialogues (especially those of Plato) are literary masterpieces; the main character in them, Socrates, was claimed by virtually every philosophical school as in some sense its founder; and the powerful impression they made on the reader would make Athens a naturally attractive setting for the study of philosophy. Second, Athens was the home of some of the most important and venerable philosophical 'schools' in the world. Indeed, the first real philosophical institution of which we have any knowledge was founded in Athens by the Athenian philosopher Plato shortly after 387 BC. Plato acquired a site less than a mile outside the gates of Athens (on the road leading from the Dipylon Gate) which was dedicated to the hero Academus (hence the school took the name 'Academy'). It apparently included a grove of trees, a garden, and a gymnasium, which would have been the setting for public lectures; legally the school may have been a *thiasos*, a religious association, dedicated to the Muses. Its activities included, besides teaching and research, religious cult and common meals. The Academy was flourishing at the time of the events narrated in *Acts*, though there is some doubt as to whether the school was continuously active throughout the intervening period; Cicero sets the 5th book of his dialogue *De Finibus* in the Academy, and represents it as being totally deserted (*De Fin.* 5, 1, 1), presumably as a result of depredations during Sulla's siege. In the 3rd century BC, there seems to have been some change in its philosophical orientation; the distinctive doctrines of Plato were, if not abandoned, then at least played down, and the public teaching of the school became sceptical in nature (perhaps as a consequence of arguments with the newly-founded Stoic and Epicurean schools). It was also very favourable to rhetoric, and so attractive to those who had in mind a career in public life (like Cicero). By the 1st century AD Platonism was having a revival, (the beginnings of a movement which would dominate philosophy, and theology, for centuries afterwards, and the source of the philosophical ideas on which the Jewish writer Philo based his interpretation of the Bible), and Ammonius, the head of the Academy at Athens at the time of, or immediately after, Paul's stay there (Plutarch has him head of the school by 67: *De E apud Delphos* 385B) was one of the leaders of that movement. The Academy continued to be active until the end of philosophical teaching at Athens in the 6th century.

From its very beginning the Academy attracted students from outside of Athens. The best known is Aristotle, from Stagira in Chalcidice (between Philippi and Thessalonica), who joined the Academy at the age of 17, and stayed there for about 20 years. He founded the next philosophical school in Athens in a gymnasium in the precinct of the god Apollo Lykeios (hence its name, the Lyceum; it was just outside the city to the east). Plato, in fact, was not only the first native-born Athenian to found a philosophical school in Athens, he was also the last; after him Athens was very much an international centre for philosophy. The Lyceum too was still in existence in the 1st century, but the distinction between its doctrines and those of the Academy at this period is not entirely clear.

Epicurus, the founder of the Epicurean school, though an Athenian citizen, was born and brought up not in Athens itself but in an Athenian settlement on Samos; when the settlers were expelled in 322 BC the family moved to Colophon; he developed most of his philosophical ideas at Mitylene and Lampsacus. But when he began to achieve international stature, he, naturally, moved to Athens (in 306 BC), and set himself up with a house and a garden (on the road leading from the Dipylon gate to the Academy). He remained there for the rest of his life.

The founder of the Stoic school, Zeno, came from Citium in Cyprus, but the school takes its name from the *stoa poikile* ('the painted stoa'), a cloister or colonnade, roofed over and open along one side, which was erected along the north edge of the *agora* in the mid-5th century BC, and is called 'painted' because in it were hung paintings on large wooden panels, by the greatest artists of the day, celebrating Athenian military prowess; the paintings were still in place at the time Paul was in Athens (Pausanias 1, 15). It was in this stoa that Zeno first taught the doctrines of Stoicism. The *stoa poikile* has been tentatively identified with a building excavated in 1981 on a site across the modern road which runs along the north side of the Agora site. The prestige of Athens as a philosophical centre meant that, besides the four major schools, it attracted adherents of schools and groups such as Cynics, Sceptics, and Neo-Pythagoreans. It should be noted, however, that an ancient philosophical school was not usually a formal institution; a group of people with similar views might agree to meet regularly in a particular place, but one could not become a member of a school in any formal sense.

The combination of philosophical and good rhetorical schools made Athens a natural destination for young men from all over the empire wishing to complete their education. The Roman orator and politician

Cicero (who spent six months there in 79 BC, during which time he attended lectures by the Epicureans Phaedrus and Zeno, and the dissident Academic Antiochus of Ascalon: *De Finibus* 1, 5, 16; 5, 1, 1), and the poet Horace (there at the outbreak of war in 42 BC) are only the best known of them. The poet Lucan (nephew of the proconsul Gallio who appears at 18.12) spent some time there (Suetonius, *Vita Lucani*).

The role of Athens as a philosophical centre was formalised by the foundation by the Emperor Marcus Aurelius of 'chairs' at Athens for each of the main philosophical schools: Stoics, Epicureans, Academics, and Peripatetics (Philostratus, *V.S.* 2, 566). The prestige they enjoyed, and the way in which they maintained the institutional continuity of their schools, is illustrated by an inscription from Athens with texts of letters of the Empress Plotina to her adoptive son Hadrian asking for permission for the current head of the Epicurean school, a Roman citizen, to make a will in Greek and to designate a non-Roman as his heir (in violation of Roman law) and to the members of the school to announce that Hadrian had agreed (E.M. Smallwood, *Documents of Nerva Trajan and Hadrian* no. 442; trans. in Lewis and Reinhold, *Roman Civilisation* II, p. 287).

Athens continued as a centre for philosophical and rhetorical teaching for centuries. In the mid-4th century AD two of the greatest Greek Christian theologians, Gregory of Nazianzus and Basil of Caesarea, spent several years there, studying under both Christian and Pagan masters. It was only when the emperor Justinian closed the pagan schools in 529 that the philosophical tradition in Athens came to an end.

Paul's preaching in Athens, the author tells us, was inspired by exasperation at seeing **how the city was full of idols** (v. 16). The word translated 'full of idols' is the Greek adjective *kateidolon*, which is found nowhere else in surviving literature, and means literally something like 'be-idolled'. R.E. Wycherley (*J. Theol. Stud.*, vol. 19 [1968] p. 619) suggested the word has been formed on the model of words like *katadendros*, 'covered in trees', and suggested the translation 'a forest of idols'. He pointed out that, at the point where a visitor who had landed at the Piraeus and come up to the city entered the Agora, the centre of public life, (that is, the north-west corner), excavation has revealed a large concentration of the pillars called *Hermai*, stylised representations of the god Hermes, which were characteristic of Athens; they might well have given the impression of a forest.

Paul naturally goes first to **the synagogue** to argue **with the Jews and Gentile worshippers** (v. 17); for Jewish-Greek inscriptions found in Attica (one dating from the 2nd century BC) see Schürer[2] III (1) p. 65. However, on this occasion he also goes to argue **in the city square every day with casual passers by** (v. 17). The 'city square' is actually the *agora* (see 16.19), the centre of Athenian public life for centuries, and full of famous monuments. Although it had once been essentially an open space surrounded by stoas (porticoes), in the Roman period new markets had been opened just to the east of the Agora, and the central space of the *agora* was occupied by grand new buildings, especially the Odeion of Agrippa. (For an account of what recent excavations have revealed of the Agora, see J. M. Camp, *The Athenian Agora*.) This is the first time we are told directly of Paul trying to evangelise Gentiles who had had no previous contact with Judaism (although it may be implied in the case of Lystra and Derbe in ch. 14).

Among those he meets are **some of the Epicurean and Stoic philosophers** (v. 18), adherents of two of the principal philosophical schools represented at Athens (see note on v. 16). The philosophical positions of these two schools were radically opposed to one another, and they were keen rivals. The Epicureans were hedonists, who believed that the end of all human endeavour was pleasure. They defined pleasure, however, as the absence of all pain, and hence all wants, and recommended a life of simple obscurity and detachment from ambition and excessive desire. They believed that the world was the creation of the random collisions of atoms, and that death was simply the extinction of the soul, and not to be feared since it was our guarantee that all pain had its limit. They believed that the gods existed, in human form, and that they spoke some form of Greek, but that, being perfect Epicureans, they cared for nothing but their own happiness, and so were totally unconcerned with the world and everything in it. They were, however, useful as models of the ideal of happiness, and the Epicureans recommended participation in normal religious cult. The Stoics were, like the Epicureans, materialists. They held that matter existed in two forms, the first of which, quality-less mass, was totally interpenetrated by the second, a creative force which gave it form, and which they called by several names, including Creative Fire, World-soul, Zeus, and God. This creative force is both purposive and beneficent, and sometimes they speak of it in language reminiscent of the ethical monotheism of the Judaeo-Christian tradition (e.g. Cleanthes, *Hymn to Zeus*), though their system is closer to Pantheism. Like most philosophers of this period, they believed that god was influenced neither by sacrifice nor by prayer, since he needed nothing and would do what was right (and only what was right) irrespective of the petitions of men. They regarded the gods of popular belief as aspects of the one divine force, or as symbols of natural forces, and interpreted mythological stories as an allegorical expression of philosophical or moral truths (some Jews, like Philo, used the same techniques in the interpretation of the Bible; from the end of the next century onwards allegorical interpretation became an important tool for Christian theologians like the Alexandrians Clement and Origen). Stoics, however, like Epicureans, approved of participation in traditional religious cults, simply because they were traditional. For the Stoics the world was created, destroyed, and recreated in an eternal succession of cycles, each of which exactly repeated every other. All things were controlled by the divine force; the individual was completely in the hands of Fate, and his only choice was whether to accept Fate's plan willingly or unwillingly. The end of life for man was to strive to be what god intended him to be, that is a properly functioning human being. They believed that this involved eliminating all non-rational elements from the soul (which they regarded as psychic disorders) and living lives of strict rectitude (though in practice the moral code they recommended was in most respects indistinguishable from that of the Epicureans).

It is interesting that Paul's speech (vv. 22-31) has many points of contact with Stoicism, but would have impressed Epicureans not at all. Later Christian thinkers and apologists seem to have found Stoicism a useful source of ideas which they could represent as being close to their own (so demonstrating that Christianity was not totally alien from the ideas of the most traditional and morally upright philosophical thinkers). Tertullian, in the early 3rd century, says of the Stoic Seneca (the brother of Gallio; see note on 18.12) that he is *saepe noster* 'often on our side' (*De An*. 20, 1); in the same century someone found it worthwhile to forge a Latin correspondence between Seneca and Paul, which indicated that Seneca had accepted Christianity and which was accepted as genuine in the 4th century (Jerome, *De Vir. Ill*. 12; Augustine *Ep*. 153, 14). The feeling does not seem to have been reciprocated; the Stoic emperor Marcus Aurelius regarded the Christians' steadfastness in the face of persecution as simple stubbornness (*Meditations* 11, 3).

Although Epicureans and Stoics were not in general at the forefront of new developments in philosophy at this period (most creative philosophical thought was Platonist in nature), they are the schools whose names the average layman would have heard. The author of *Acts* shows no knowledge of philosophy at all; the important thing for him is that Paul encounters philosophers in Athens, the city which was at the very heart of pagan philosophy.

The philosophers (for no one else is mentioned as participating) believe Paul to be **a propagandist for foreign deities – this because he was preaching about Jesus and Resurrection** (v. 18). The *NEB* translation assumes that the philosophers have misunderstood the words 'Jesus' and 'Resurrection' (Greek *anastasis*) as names of foreign gods. This is a possible, but not an inevitable, interpretation. A foreign name, and the mention of rising from the dead, would be enough to show the listeners that some foreign cult was involved. It has been argued that the reference to introducing 'foreign deities' is intended to bring to the reader's mind the accusation against Socrates, who was tried and put to death in Athens in 399 BC on charges which included 'introducing new gods' (Haenchen, p.

518; cf. BC IV, p. 212). There is not, however, a precise parallel between the two cases (compare Xenophon, *Mem.* 1, 1, 1, and Plato, *Apology* 24B). Both Plato and Xenophon were widely read in antiquity, and the story of Socrates would be known, at least in its outlines, to anyone whose education had gone beyond the most elementary level (and note that the author expects his readers to pick up two unattributed quotations to classical poets in Paul's speech), so it would be reasonable to expect that at least some of the readers of *Acts* could be expected to see, and be intrigued by, such similarities as there are between the situations of Socrates and Paul. On the other hand, the two cases are fundamentally different (Socrates was a citizen, while Paul was a foreigner; Socrates is accused of introducing 'new' or 'other' gods, Paul of preaching 'foreign' gods), and the similarities cannot be used as the basis of an argument that Paul is being set up as a sort of Christian Socrates.

So they took him and brought him before the Court of Areopagus (*NEB*) *or* **they took hold of him and brought him to the Areopagus** (*RSV*; v. 19), and ask him to explain what he is teaching. The motive given by the author is curiosity: **the Athenians in general and the foreigners there had no time for anything but talking or hearing about the latest novelty** (v. 21); the 'foreigners' would include tourists, students, and other visitors drawn to Athens by its cultural traditions; many would be from the highest ranks of society.

This passage has given rise to lively controversy, and the two translations quoted are based on opposed understandings of what was going on. Were it not for the mention of the Areopagus, we would have no reason to believe other than that the philosophers wished to hear what Paul has to say, and invited him to a suitable location where he could give an account of his beliefs; this indeed is the sort of thing which philosophers came to the *agora* to do. When he has spoken, some are still interested, and others think he is talking nonsense (v. 32) and the meeting breaks up. The problem is that the site of the Areopagus (literally, the 'Hill of Ares') is a most unsuitable place to hold a discussion (Haenchen, p. 518). It is a rocky crag, really an outcrop of the Acropolis, at the south-west corner of the *agora*. Although in Paul's day anyone ascending the hill would not run the risks faced by modern visitors of slipping and injuring themselves on the rock worn smooth by generations of pious tourists hoping to stand where Paul preached, foundations carved in the rock do indicate that in antiquity it was covered in some sort of structures, and, in any case, why take the trouble to climb up to this cramped and inconvenient location, when the *agora* was surrounded by spacious, cool, and shady *stoas* put up for the express purpose of creating a pleasant environment where people could meet and talk? (One of them, the Stoa of Attalus, was completely reconstructed in 1956 to house the Agora Museum; it gives the visitor a very vivid impression of what a pleasant place the *agora* might have been in antiquity.) However, the name had also come to be used for an institution, a body formally entitled 'the Council from the Areopagus' (because it had originally met there), but commonly known simply as 'the Areopagus'. Without a clear topographical reference, a reader who was familiar with Athens would assume that a reference to the Areopagus would apply to the Council. Such a reader might, with the events of Philippi in his mind, assume that Paul had been seized and taken before the Council for some kind of trial. But how familiar would the author of *Acts* assume that his readers were with the details of civic government in Athens? The verb in the phrase translated 'they took him' (*epilabomenoi*) is used in *Acts* of a physical seizure in a hostile sense (16.19; 18.17; 21.30), but it is also used when Barnabas takes Paul to the apostles (9.27), and when Claudius Lysias takes Paul's nephew to one side to hear his information (23.19).

The Council of the Areopagus did perform the same function in Athens as the *duoviri* at Philippi, or the politarchs at Thessalonica. It acted as the chief executive of the city, and was the body before which a complaint of impiety against a visitor would be brought in the first instance. It was very unusual indeed (probably unique) for the executive functions in any city of the empire to be performed by any body large enough to be called a Council, whose members served for life, rather than by a small group of officers elected annually (see Introduction p. 17). Nevertheless it is clear that this was the case at Athens from the formula used by emperors in their epistles to the city of Athens. The standard formula used for most Greek cities was 'to the archons, the *Boule* (Council), and the *Demos* (People) of the -ians, greetings', but for Athens the formula used was 'to the *Boule* from the Areopagus, the *Boule* of 600 (later 500), and the *Demos* of the Athenians, greetings' (see, e.g. E.M. Smallwood, *Documents of Nerva, Trajan, and Hadrian*, no. 445, ll. 7-9). The other evidence of the Areopagus' power, especially as the chief court at Athens, is assembled by Barnes (*J. Theol. Stud.* vol. 20, pp. 411-13; see also Geagan, *The Athenian Constitution after Sulla*). Discussion of this passage in most existing commentaries is vitiated by disregard of this evidence and the assumption that the drastic reduction in the Areopagus' powers when a full democracy was established at Athens in 462 BC was the last significant event in the Council's history.

Barnes is therefore able to argue that Paul was indeed put on trial before the Areopagus: he dismisses the objection that there was no formal accusation or verdict because 'this argument...appears to presuppose an anachronistic notion of what constitutes a criminal trial' (art. cit., p. 413). The complaint made by those who brought Paul to the Council was that he was trying to persuade Athenians to worship foreign gods (vv. 18-20). Here, Barnes' comment on how the later persecutions of Christians arose is apposite: 'once it was realised Christianity entailed abandoning established cult, Christians could expect little sympathy' (*JRS*, vol. 58 [1968] pp. 49ff.). Elements in the speech put in Paul's mouth are interpreted by Barnes as an answer to this charge.

So it is possible that Paul faced a trial at Athens. There are nevertheless problems with this view. Were it not for the mention of the Areopagus, combined with the improbability of leaving the *agora* and climbing the hill simply to have a discussion, the question of a trial would never arise. The people initially concerned were philosophers, but there is no reason why they in particular should have wanted to report Paul to the authorities; it is improbable that there was a philosophical 'closed shop' at Athens and no motives of professional jealousy or malice are alleged (contrast the action of the silversmiths at Ephesus: 19.24-7). Indeed, the motive for the discussion is explicitly said to have been curiosity (vv. 20-1). In fact, the course of the episode is closely parallel with the incident at Pisidian Antioch where Paul preaches in the synagogue. In both cases, he is invited to speak by people of some significance in that community: philosophers at Athens (17.18); the leaders of the synagogue at Antioch (13.15). In each case he opens his speech with an account of religion which his hearers will find familiar: God's dealings with Israel at Antioch, God the creator (without any biblical references) at Athens. The resurrection of Jesus is represented as the beginning of a new era. The message gets a mixed reception (13.43-5; 17.32). The outcome is converts (13.48; 17.33-4). Whether this was a trial or not, it does look as if, just as we are offered the speech at Pisidian Antioch as a representative sample of Paul's preaching to Jews and 'god-fearers', so his speech in Athens represents his approach to Gentiles with no knowledge of Judaism. It is, of course, not surprising that a speech like this contains material which could also have been used as part of a defence against an accusation of impiety. It is hard to understand why the author leaves us to infer a trial from the context only in the very city whose unique constitutional arrangements would be most likely to have been misunderstood by non-Athenian readers. It is also strange if the author, who misses no other opportunity to point out to us that charges against the Christians brought before properly constituted authorities were, if properly investigated, found to be groundless (18.14-15; 26.32), should not have told us here if an accusation against Paul had failed.

Where then would the Areopagus Council have met? Barnes argues that the Council still held its meetings on the hill, so that 'the Areopagus' here refers both to the institution and to the site (art. cit. pp. 409-10). Yet there is evidence that the Council sometimes met in the *Stoa Basileios* (the King's Portico, named because it was used in the classical period by the officer known as 'the King', one of the archons responsible in particular for religious matters, including homicide, and who had been in the 5th and

4th centuries BC the president of the Council of the Areopagus, and may well still have been so in Paul's day; this is the setting for Plato's dialogue *Euthyphro*, which takes place when Socrates is awaiting the preliminary processes before the King in preparation for his trial). It has been identified with a small building at the northern end of the west side of the *agora*, where it forms the north-western corner with the *Stoa Poikile*, a regular haunt of philosophers. It would, then, be a convenient place to take a stranger to hear what he has to say for himself, whether for a formal trial, or for a discussion in the presence of the Council, who were exercising a general oversight of public order and morals, or simply for curiosity.

There is no final way of deciding between these hypotheses. For an extensive bibliography on the whole question of Paul's Areopagus speech, see Bruce, pp. 379-80.

The speech itself is very appropriate for a Gentile audience, since it not only contains no biblical references (but it does have two quotations from pagan authors: vv. 27-8), but there is actually no explicit Jewish or Christian content until we get to v. 31. Much of the speech is a compilation of philosophical commonplaces, to which his audience would have found no objection.

Paul begins with a reference to **an altar bearing the inscription 'To an Unknown God'** (v. 23) – the God which he will now proclaim to them. There is a good deal of evidence, both literary and epigraphic, from Attica and other parts of the Greek world, for the erection of altars dedicated to 'gods unknown' in the plural, but no certain parallel for an altar to a single 'god unknown'. See Wycherley, *J. Theol. Stud.* vol. 19, pp. 620-1, for a hypothesis about how such cults came into existence in the area of the Agora: when prehistoric burials were disturbed permanent cults were sometimes established; some would become attached to a name or legend, but others would remain 'nameless' (but strictly speaking these would be cults of 'heroes', not of gods).

Of the points Paul makes in his speech, the first, that God is the creator of all things (v. 24) would have been accepted by all philosophical schools except the Epicureans (who argued that the world came about through the random collisions of atoms); similarly, there would have been general agreement that gods are not restricted to temples and images (v. 24). That God needs nothing (v. 25) was an old philosophical idea (e.g. Plato, *Euthyphro* 15A); that men are **of one stock** (v. 26) was a view held by the Stoics, and before them by the Cynics; the phrase **he fixed the epochs of their history** (v. 26) may actually refer to the seasons of the year, unless it is an appeal to Stoic theories of the inexorable progress of each cosmic cycle. A later commentary on *Acts* claims that the phrase **in him we live and move, in him we exist** (v. 27) is a quotation from a poem by the Cretan Epimenides (see Bruce p. 384). There is an explicit quotation in the next verse: **we are also his offspring** (v. 28), which is part of l. 5 of the *Phainomena* of Aratus, a strange (and not entirely accurate) work written in the 3rd century BC on the positions of the stars; it was curiously popular in antiquity, and frequently read in schools (H.I. Marrou, *A History of Education in Antiquity*, pp. 184-5). Though it is by no means impossible that Paul (or the author of *Acts*) had read these works, it is more probable that these quotations came from an anthology or a collection of *doxai* (views of distinguished authors on various topics). The sentiments of the verses quoted are very much in line with Stoicism. Paul concludes with a call to repentance (v. 31).

The result of Paul's activity in Athens is two converts: Damaris (of whom nothing is known) and **Dionysius, a member of the court of Areopagus** (v. 34). Dionysius' membership of the Areopagus Council has been taken as evidence that Paul had addressed the Council. It is mentioned here, however, because it signifies that he enjoyed the highest social position, and *Acts* tends to go out of its way to draw our attention to converts and supporters from the social elite (like the Asiarchs in 19.31). According to Eusebius (*Ecclesiastical History* 3, 4, 11) he was the first bishop of Athens, but he achieved wider fame as the supposed author of a considerable body of theological writings strongly influenced by later Neoplatonism produced, perhaps in Syria, probably in the 5th century, which had considerable influence on the development of theology and philosophy in the middle ages. He was later confused with a 3rd century Gallic martyr, and became St Denis, the patron saint of France.

Chapter 18

Paul travels to Corinth; he is brought before the governor, who declines to take action against him; he travels to Ephesus, where he meets Apollos.

Corinth (v. 1), Paul's next destination, was originally an ancient Greek *polis*, but it had been destroyed (i.e. the population killed or enslaved, the territory confiscated, the town left in ruins, and the existence of the state terminated) in 146 BC by Rome, after the defeat of the Achaean League to which the city had belonged. The site was used by Julius Caesar in 46 BC for the establishment of a Roman citizen colony named *Colonia Laus Julia Corinthus*. It is described in commentaries and textbooks as the 'capital' of the province of Achaia (created in 27 BC) or as the 'headquarters' of its proconsul; see note on 17.1 for the difficulty of making sense of such concepts.

In Corinth Paul meets **a Jew named Aquila, a native of Pontus, and his wife Priscilla** who had **recently arrived from Italy because Claudius** had issued an edict that all Jews should leave Rome (v. 2). Both Aquila and Priscilla have Latin names, and Aquila (= eagle) could well have been the 'family name' (*cognomen*) of a Roman citizen (see Introduction pp. 25-6). It has been argued that the fact that Aquila came from the remote area of Pontus (the south coast of the Black Sea) makes it doubtful that he really was a citizen (Sherwin-White [1963] pp. 158-9); but Paul was a citizen, though he was a Jew from Tarsus in Cilicia, a region which could also be regarded as remote. The reference to the edict of Claudius raises great difficulties over chronology. Paul's arrival in Corinth can be dated to 49 or 50, because of the evidence of vv. 11-12 (see notes). The stress on the word 'recently' would lead the reader to assume that Claudius' expulsion order dated from the year 49. There is evidence in other sources for such an order, but they appear to be in disagreement about its date.

1: Suetonius, *Claudius* 25, 4: 'He expelled from Rome Jews who were making constant disturbances at the instigation of Chrestus.' Suetonius does not date this event, and there is no way of deciding the hotly-debated issue of whether he has garbled a source which referred to troubles provoked by the arrival of Christian evangelists at Rome; the presence of Christians at Rome would have been far more likely in 49 than as early as 41 (see point 2 below). Is Chrestus a misspelling of Christus and did Suetonius assume that Chrestus/Christus was alive and in Rome during the disturbances (which is described by E.M. Smallwood, *The Jews under Roman Rule*, pp. 210ff. as 'the only reasonable view'; cf. Bruce *Bull. John Ryl. Lib.* vol. 44, p. 316; S. Safai and M. Stern, *The Jewish People in the First Century* vol. 1, pp. 180-2)? However, Suetonius is likely to have been too well informed to do this; he dealt with the persecution of 64 in his life of Nero (16, 2), and may well have been present when Pliny interrogated the Christians of Pontus (Williams, *Pliny: Correspondence with Trajan from Bithynia*, pp. 87, 137, 139-44).

2: Dio Cassius, in the course of narrating the events of the year of Claudius' accession, 41 (60, 6, 6), reports that the emperor first planned to expel all Jews from Rome, but then, because they were so numerous that the expulsion could not be carried out without disturbance, forbade them to assemble for any gatherings.

3: The Christian historian Orosius (7, 6, 15) says that Josephus records that the Jews were expelled from Rome in Claudius' ninth year (i.e. 49) and he also quotes Suetonius' words; but there is no such report in the surviving works of Josephus (and they appear to have survived in their entirety).

It has been argued that there were two separate decisions by Claudius about the Jews of Rome, a ban on meetings in 41, and an expulsion in 49. However, apart from this verse in *Acts*, there is no evidence for an expulsion in 49 except Orosius' dating of the expulsion mentioned by Suetonius, and his mistaken reference to Josephus shows that Orosius' chronology is quite unreliable. A strong argument against an expulsion in 49 is the silence of Tacitus who did record a similar event in Tiberius' reign in his *Annals* (2, 85); Tacitus' narrative of the year 41 is lost but that for 49 is extant. The most straightforward solution is to suppose that all the references are to a single event, which is most fully described and correctly dated by Dio Cassius. In that case the author of *Acts* was mistaken either in saying that Aquila and Priscilla had 'recently' come from Italy, or in linking their arrival in Corinth with Claudius' expulsion order (Stern, loc. cit., suggested they could have moved from Rome to some other part of Italy in 41 and thence to Corinth some years later).

Paul **made his home with them, and they carried on business together; they were tentmakers** (v. 3). The word 'tentmaker' (Greek *skenopoios*) is used generally to mean 'leather-worker' (BC IV, p. 223; ancient tents were usually made of leather). Paul writes to the Thessalonians (1 Thess. 2.9): 'we worked for a living night and day, rather than be a burden to anyone, while we proclaimed before you the good news of God'. As usual, he begins by teaching **in the synagogue Sabbath by Sabbath** (v. 4; for other evidence of Jews in Corinth see Schürer[2] III [1] pp. 65-6), but when he meets with opposition he announces; **I shall go to the Gentiles** (v. 6), and moves **to the house of a worshipper of God named Titius Iustus** (v. 7), who is presumably a Gentile 'god-fearer', so moving into his house would be a symbolic act of rejection. Titius and Iustus are wholly convincing as the clan-name and family-name of a Roman citizen (which a citizen of the colony of Corinth would automatically be: Sherwin-White [1963] p. 158). If Iustus is identical with the Gaius referred to by Paul in 1 Cor. 1.14 as the only Corinthian he had baptised apart from Crispus, he had a full set of *tria nomina* (see Introduction pp. 25-6). **Crispus, who held office in the synagogue** (v. 8) is actually the *archisynagogos* (see note on 13.15). He himself was baptised by Paul (1 Cor 1.14). Although a Jew he had a common Roman family-name (*cognomen*) meaning 'curly-haired'.

Trouble breaks out, and Paul is brought to court by the Jews before **Gallio...proconsul of Achaia** (v. 12). The province of Achaia, which included southern and central Greece, was called *Achaia* in Latin, rather than *Graecia*, because the greater part of it, in the Peloponnese, had comprised the territory of the federal republic of Achaea, defeated and dismembered by Rome in 146 BC. Lucius Junius Gallio was a member of a very distinguished Roman family of this period. His original name was Lucius Annaeus Novatus, as son of M. Annaeus Seneca of Cordoba (author of works on rhetoric) and hence brother both of Lucius Seneca, who composed philosophical works and tragedies and who was Nero's chief adviser from 54-62, and of Annaeus Mela, father of the poet Lucan. He was probably adopted by a senator named Junius Gallio. One of his brother's *Epistles* (104, 1) attests his presence in Achaia, and a fragmentary Greek inscription from Delphi confirms the allusion in *Acts* to his proconsulship and makes it possible to date his one-year term (one year was standard for all proconsuls).

The definitive publication of this inscription is that by A. Plassart as *Fouilles de Delphes* III (iv) no. 286 (which followed his article in *Revue des Etudes Grecques* vol. 80 [1967] pp. 372-8; see also the text published by J.H. Oliver, *Hesperia* vol. 40 [1971] pp. 239-40). The text was a pronouncement in Greek by the emperor Claudius, at a time when he had been saluted as *imperator* (victorious general) for the 26th time, but not yet for the 27th (which had certainly happened before August 1, 52); that was probably in the early months of 52. Before Plassart's publications the text had been interpreted as an epistle of Claudius to the city of Delphi. In the text, Claudius referred to L. Junius Gallio, 'my friend, and proconsul'. It was assumed that Gallio was therefore in office as proconsul late in 51 or early 52. Plassart argued that the epistle was addressed to Gallio's successor as proconsul, but this interpretation should be rejected; it depends purely on the way in which five Greek letters on an incomplete part of the inscription are divided up into words (see Oliver, art. cit.); and in any case an epistle to a proconsul would have been written in Latin; and, had a copy been supplied to the city of Delphi, it would not have reproduced the emperor's full titles.

Gallio's year as proconsul probably fell in the later part of 51 and the early part of 52, so that Paul's arrival in Corinth, a year and a half before his trial (v. 11), happened late in 49 or in early or middle 50.

The Jews set upon Paul and brought him into court or, more literally with *RSV*, **before the tribunal** (v. 12). The *tribunal* (in Greek *bema*) was an elevated platform (cf. note on 12.21). The author of *Acts* uses the correct term for the place where a proconsul administered justice in public; and also correct procedure, arrest by private prosecutors (see note on 16.20-1). The charge is **inducing people to worship God in ways that are against the law** (v. 13). Phrased in this way it is ambiguous, and Gallio, perhaps disingenuously, exploits the ambiguity to avoid dealing with it (Sherwin-White [1963] pp. 99-107). 'The law' is imprecise; is this Jewish law or Roman law? To worship 'god' (in the singular) implies an offence against Jewish law, since a Roman would have said 'the gods'. On the other hand, 'people' is a much wider category than 'Jews'. Sherwin-White (1963) points out that at Corinth (as at Philippi) it would have been appropriate for the charge 'persuading Romans contrary to Roman law' to be presented to a Roman proconsul; yet it would be very odd for Jews to do this, and indeed there was no recent tradition of enforcing religious conformity upon Romans (see note to 16.20-1). On the other hand there is no evidence that any binding precedent required Roman governors to help the leaders of Jewish congregations enforce religious orthodoxy on dissident Jews such as Paul (cf. note on 9.2; Sherwin-White [1963] loc. cit.; Schürer² III [1] pp. 118-20). However, as Sherwin-White (1963) stressed (pp. 14ff.; 99ff.), a governor had great discretion to entertain novel criminal charges, so it was worth the while of the Jews of Corinth to 'try it on' with Gallio; they were just unlucky in their governor.

Gallio rejects the charge out of hand (v. 14); governors had the discretion to do this and, since he was probably under pressure to deal with a great deal of judicial business, he had a powerful motive for doing so. An impetuous decision would be in character for Gallio, to judge by the tone of his brother Seneca's words (*Ep.* 104, 1): 'that remark of my lord Gallio's, who, when he had contracted a fever in Achaia, *at once* went on board ship, exclaiming that it was a sickness not of his body, but of the place'. But he does give a reason for his dismissal of the charge which would have been entirely convincing from a Roman point of view: **if it is some bickering about words and names and your Jewish law, you may see to it yourselves** (v. 15). He seizes on the ambiguity of the reference to 'the law' to justify rejecting the complaint; only offences against Roman law are his concern. The tone of disdain in his response would fit in with the contempt (rather than active hostility) towards Judaism common among educated Romans of the period, to judge by Latin literature of the age (see: Schürer² III [1] pp. 152-3; Sherwin-White, *Racial Prejudice in Imperial Rome*, ch. 3; S. Safrai and M. Stern, *The Jewish People in the First Century*, vol. 2, pp. 1101-58). Whether 'see to it yourselves' should be interpreted as an actual invitation to the Jews to inflict punishment on Paul is unclear; Lake and Cadbury hold that it implied 'not so much a command to another as the speaker's renunciation of his own responsibility' (BC IV, p. 228).

The immediate outcome is a fracas before the *tribunal*: **there was a general attack on Sosthenes, who held office in the synagogue, and they gave him a beating in full view of the bench** (v. 17). Sosthenes, like Crispus (v. 8) is said to be an *archisynagogos*. Commentators are divided between two interpretations of this incident: (A): Sosthenes was a Christian, an associate of Paul, and was beaten by the Jewish delegation; (B): Sosthenes was the leader of that delegation and was beaten by the Gentile bystanders (Bruce, p. 397; Haenchen, pp. 536-7; Lake and Cadbury, BC

IV, p. 228, suggest the Jews joined in because Sosthenes had mismanaged the case). The ambiguity implicit in 'general' (more literally translated 'all') was noticed by the editor of the 'Western' text, who inserted 'all the Greeks', and the alternative interpretation was championed by the scribes of some manuscripts who emended this to 'all the Jews' (BC IV, p. 228).

In favour of (A) is the fact that the last group to be mentioned are the members of the Jewish delegation, and that a Sosthenes appears as a companion of Paul in 1 *Corinthians* 1.1 (but that need not mean that he was a native of Corinth; and it could just be a coincidence of names). In favour of (B) is the fact that the reader would assume that an *archisynagogos* who is not explicitly described as a Christian convert (as Crispus was, v. 8) was the leader of the Jewish delegation to Gallio; furthermore, if the Jews had beaten up anyone, it would surely have been Paul. The balance of probability seems to be in favour of (B). The evidence of hostility among urban Greeks towards Jewish minorities (notably at Alexandria) makes it entirely credible that a Gentile crowd would take the proconsul's reaction to the Jews as a signal for indulging in some 'Jew-bashing'.

The comment that **all this left Gallio quite unconcerned** (v. 17) clearly implies that Gallio was still present on the *tribunal* when the beating took place in front of his eyes. The 'Western' text altered it to read 'Gallio pretended not to see'. It may seem surprising that a Roman governor, even if contemptuous of Jews, should tolerate such disorder in his own presence and not feel it was an insult to his own dignity. However, every governor was a law to himself. For an example of idiosyncratic behaviour, compare the anecdote in Tertullian (*Ad Scap.* 5) about Arrius Antoninus, proconsul of Asia in the late 2nd century; when faced by a crowd of Christians volunteering for martyrdom, after having some executed, he said to the rest: 'You wretches, if you want to die you can use nooses or cliffs'.

After staying at Corinth for some time, Paul makes for Antioch, pausing at **Cenchreae** where **he had his hair cut off, because he was under a vow** (v. 18). Cenchreae was the site of the harbour on the southern side of the Isthmus of Corinth, about seven miles from the city itself; it would be the point of departure for travellers going east by sea. The significance of the vow which leads Paul to cut his hair is unclear. *Numbers* 6.1-21 sets out the terms of the oath taken by a 'Nazirite' 'to separate himself to the Lord'; they include: 'All the days of his vow of separation no razor shall come upon his head...he shall let the locks of his head grow long' (v. 6). The problem in interpreting this incident as the conclusion of a Nazirite vow is that the hair should be cut only in Jerusalem. It may have been the fulfilment of some private vow. This vow is sometimes held to be inconsistent with the attitudes expressed by Paul in his letters.

He lands at **Ephesus** (v. 19), a very ancient Greek city on the eastern coast of Asia Minor. In the Roman period it was one of the largest and wealthiest cities in the province of Asia, engaged in fierce contention with its rivals Smyrna and Pergamum over titles of honour (see notes to 19.23-40 for more details of its institutions). It was not, as is sometimes said (Haenchen p. 543) the capital of the province or the place of residence of the governor (see notes to 17.1 and 18.1). For the **synagogue** (v. 19) see Schürer[2] III (1) pp. 22-3.

His next destination is **Caesarea** (v. 22; see note on 10.1) from where **he went up and paid his respects to the church, and then went down to Antioch** (v. 22). The reference to 'going up' must surely indicate that this is a visit to Jerusalem. The Greek verb is used for journeys inland and 'up country' from the coast, but Jerusalem is both inland and in hill country.

After Antioch, **he set out again and made a journey through the Galatian country and on through Phrygia** (v. 23). The Greek phrase used here makes it clear that, unlike 16.6, two separate geographical areas are meant. Paul went in turn through (i) the Galatian country and (ii) Phrygia. Haenchen (p. 545) says it is unclear why Phrygia is named second here and first in 16.6. But if in 16.6 what is being referred to is a single area (see note on 16.6), while two distinct areas are being alluded to here, the explanation is clear: the two areas are mentioned in the chronological order in which Paul reached them. A journey overland from Antioch in Syria (v. 22) to Ephesus (19.1) would take Paul across Asia Minor from east to west; the obvious route would be along the line of the old Persian 'Royal Road', north through the Cilician Gates and then west along the southern edge of the central Anatolian plateau. Such a route would take him through (in order from east to west) Derbe, Lystra, Iconium, and Antioch; hence the words **bringing new strength to all the converts** (v. 23; cf. 13.14-14.22 and 16.1-6). All four cities lay in the *province* of Galatia; so 'Galatian country' could refer to all of them, and 'Phrygia' to the eastern part of the province of Asia (the 'inland regions' of 19.1) through which he would have to pass on his way to Ephesus. But the word order should imply that there were already disciples in both districts (and Col. 2.1 shows that Paul had not visited churches in the interior of Asia in existence in his day, at Hierapolis, Laodicea, and Colossae), so 'Galatian country' should refer to Derbe, Lystra, and, perhaps, Iconium, and Phrygia to 'Pisidian' Antioch and, perhaps, Iconium (see notes on 13.14 and 14.1). What this interpretation rules out is a visit to the parts of northern Anatolia where the Galatian language was spoken (Haenchen p. 548); to visit that area while on the way from Syrian Antioch to Ephesus and before visiting Phrygia Paul would have had to take a very circuitous route north-east from the Cilician gates through Cappadocia to skirt the semi-desert 'treeless plain' (*Axylon* in Greek) of central Anatolia. Even if churches existed in 'linguistic Galatia' (and this is the hypothesis for which the alternative interpretation of this verse is itself supposed to be evidence!), the more obvious route would be to go to Iconium and Antioch (i.e. 'Phrygia') first, and then north and north-east (west of the *Axylon*).

The narrative now moves to Ephesus, where we are introduced to **a Jew named Apollos, an Alexandrian by birth** (v. 24). Alexandria was the largest and most famous of the Greek cities named after Alexander the Great. Alexandria 'next to Egypt' was the home of the largest Jewish Diaspora community until the revolt of AD 116-17 (see Schürer[2] III [1] pp. 42-4).

This is one of the few glimpses we are given in *Acts* of vigorous missionary activity going on independently of the events which *Acts* describes. Apollos **knew only John's baptism** (v. 25), and not the baptism of Jesus, which seems to involve the gift of the Holy Spirit marked by ecstatic speech (see note on 19.5-6). No doubt, then, 'John's baptism' was simple baptism in water (see note on 8.12). We are not told by what route Apollos became a Christian, or in what, until he is enlightened by Priscilla and Aquila, his Christianity consisted. He clearly became an important figure in the beginnings of Christianity; Paul tells us (1 Cor. 1.12) that some Christians at Corinth regarded themselves as followers of Apollos. Paul and Apollos do not meet at this stage, though they do later (1 Cor. 16.12); Apollos departs **to Achaia** (v. 27) (i.e. Corinth; see 19.1), before Paul arrives at Ephesus.

Chapter 19

Paul comes to Ephesus; his preaching causes a riot which is controlled with difficulty.

Paul's journey **through the inland regions** (v. 1) could cover the whole of Paul's route back to Ephesus. For **John's baptism** (v. 3) see note to 18.25. When the rebaptised converts receive the gift of the Spirit and begin to speak **in tongues of ecstasy** (v. 6) the reference is probably to the sort of phenomenon Paul experienced at Corinth (1 Cor. 14.1-25), speaking in incomprehensible tongues, rather than the miraculous gift of languages the apostles received at Pentecost (see notes to 2.6 and 10.46).

Once back in Ephesus, Paul, having been rejected by the synagogue, instead holds **discussions daily in the lecture-hall of Tyrannus** (v. 9). The Greek word translated 'lecture-hall' is *schole* (the root of the English word 'school'). Originally it meant 'leisure', then 'talk', especially a learned discussion. Here it must be a building for such discussion. Nothing is known about Tyrannus (though, since we are not told otherwise, presumably he was a Gentile). As a result of Paul's teaching, **the whole popula-**

tion of the province of Asia (v. 10), we are told, heard the message. Asia was the Roman name for a large province covering what is now western Turkey, formed from the territories bequeathed to Rome in 133 BC by King Attalus III of Pergamum. (See Col. 2.1 and 4.13 for three churches founded in the Lycus valley in Asia, but not visited by Paul.)

Paul's success, not just as a preacher, but also as a healer and exorcist, encourages other exorcists to use the name of Jesus in their exorcisms. One group, the **seven sons of Sceva, a Jewish chief priest** (v. 14) are over-powered by an evil spirit which they try to cast out in the name of Jesus. No person with the name of Sceva, or anything comparable, was High Priest in this period; if the text here is sound, then presumably this was a fraudulent claim to boost their status as exorcists (BC IV, p. 241; Bruce, p. 411). Many then came and **confessed that they had been using magical spells** (v. 18); a bonfire is made of books of magic up to the value of **fifty thousand pieces of silver** (v. 20). There was a vast literature of magic in antiquity, some of which survives on papyrus. Ephesus seems to have been a particularly important centre for magic: Plutarch *Quaest. Conviv.* 7, 706E.

Paul now makes his plans for the future: he will **visit Macedonia and Achaia and then go on to Jerusalem** (v. 21); afterwards he determines that he will **see Rome also** (v. 21). The rest of *Acts* is about the completion of that programme.

The episode in the report that **about that time, the Christian move-ment gave rise to a serious disturbance** (v. 23) is not closely linked to the narrative of Paul's own experiences. Indeed, Paul seems not to have been involved at all; the only reference to him in the story itself is in a kind of parenthesis (vv. 30-1), which explains his *absence* from the meeting in the theatre, although Demetrius in his speech makes Paul's preaching the cause of the conversions which have reduced the silversmiths' income (v. 26). Hence Dibelius maintained that the episode did not belong to 'the accounts about Paul' (*Studies in Acts*, p. 211, n. 12). The Greek word translated 'disturbance', *tarachos*, means a virtual riot. The same word in its feminine form, *tarache*, occurs in an edict of a proconsul of Asia of uncertain date, part of which is preserved on an inscription from Ephesus. It deals with demonstrations by bakers from Ephesus who had withdrawn their labour: 'so that it comes about that sometimes the people fall into tumult and clamours because of the insolent assembling of bakers in the *agora*' (trans. from the text of R. Merkelbach, *Zeitschr. f. Papyrol. u. Epigraphik* 30, p. 164, ll. 1-3; for the rest of the text, see note on v. 40).

The riot is stirred up by **a man named Demetrius, a silversmith who made silver shrines of Diana and provided a great deal of employment for the craftsmen** (v. 24). Diana (or more properly Artemis) of Ephesus seems to have been originally a non-Greek (perhaps local) goddess, with little in common with the Artemis of Greece, the virgin huntress. She is normally represented with rows of protuberances across her chest, which have been interpreted as, among other things, breasts, eggs, dates, aubergines, and bulls' testicles; numerous animals are portrayed on her lower limbs. Her head priest, a eunuch and always non-Greek, had the un-Greek title 'Megabyxus', meaning in Persian 'set free by god' or 'given by god'. She was served by a body of virgin priestesses, and (among others) twenty *acrobatae*, 'walkers on tiptoe'. She was an exotic goddess, with a cult quite different from what was usual elsewhere in the Greek world. Her cult-image was housed in her famous temple, and numerous copies of it have survived. Many miniature copies in terracotta were produced at Ephesus, presumably as souvenirs for pilgrims. It has been suggested that the 'shrines' referred to here are in fact *aediculae*, miniature shrines containing copies of the cult-image (see M. Henig, *Handbook of Roman Art*, p. 148 and 194); the image would be of greater concern to the pilgrims than the actual temple. Such copies in silver are, of course, liable to be melted down in later centuries, and so do not survive, unlike cheap terracotta. A benefactor of Ephesus in AD 104 provided for a full-scale silver copy of the image to be made and set up in the theatre at each meeting of the *ekklesia* (OGIS no. 480, ll. 6-9).

How Demetrius, himself a silversmith, provided his fellow craftsmen with 'a great deal of employment' is unclear. He is unlikely to have been the owner/manager of a large workshop with enough 'employees' to form a crowd. Such 'factories' were virtually unknown in the urban crafts of the classical world, and workshops which required more labour than the master's family could provide were manned by slaves. The craftsmen are thus likely to have been 'self-employed' silversmiths. Possibly Demetrius coordinated the production of standardised images in silver by a large number of small craftsmen; he may have been rich enough to lend them the raw material in advance. The author is perhaps being a touch cynical in attributing the disturbance purely to commercial motives; religious feeling was genuine in antiquity, and a slight to a god or goddess could arouse strong feelings; if the deity was a local one (note that the rioters shout their support for Diana *of the Ephesians*, not just any Diana), then local patriotism too would be involved.

Demetrius **called a meeting of these men** (v. 25); this sort of gathering in towns was frowned on by the Roman authorities because they were likely to lead to disturbances (as indeed they did in this case). The proconsul's edict quoted in the note to v. 23 referred to a gathering (*syllogos*) of the bakers, and the emperor Trajan in a letter to Pliny, governor of Bithynia-Pontus ca. 110-12, expressed a fear that 'such a gathering would be used to form crowds and unlawful assemblies' (Pliny, *Epistles* 10, 93). Demetrius claims not only that Paul's preaching will affect the trade in graven images, but also that there is a risk **that the sanctuary of the great goddess Diana will cease to command respect; and then it will not be long before she who is worshipped by all Asia and the civilised world is brought down from her divine pre-eminence** (v. 27). The actual structure of the sanctuary mentioned, the temple of Artemis at Ephesus, was one of the Seven Wonders of the World; the temple of Paul's day had been built in the 4th century BC to replace an earlier temple destroyed by fire; the site of the temple, on flat marshy ground outside the city, was re-discovered by a British engineer, J.T. Wood, in the 1870s; the remains on the site today are unimpressive and rather sad, but parts of the masonry on display in the British Museum give a sense of the size and grandeur of the temple in antiquity. The temple was also of great importance as an institution. The goddess owned extensive estates (Rostovtzeff, *Social and Economic History of the Roman Empire*, p. 656, n. 6). The temple was also one of only a small number of shrines in the entire empire which were permitted by decisions of emperors or of the Senate to become heirs under Roman wills (*Tituli Ulpiani* 22, 6). Demetrius' claims for the world-wide worship of the goddess were repeated in a decree of the city of Ephesus about a century later: 'the goddess Artemis who presides over our city is honoured not only in her own native land...but also among Greeks and barbarians, so that everywhere shrines and precincts are consecrated, and altars are founded to her because of her vivid epiphanies' (*Sylloge*, no. 867, ll. 29ff.). Among the numerous pieces of evidence which confirm these assertions one striking example is the coin of Eumeneia in the interior of Asia Minor which carries a representation of the temple of Ephesian Artemis (M.J. Price and B.L. Trell, *Coins and their Cities*, p. 33 and colour plate 32 on p. 120).

As a result of Demetrius' speech the people **were roused to fury** (v. 28), and Paul's companions **the Macedonians Gaius and Aristarchus** are seized and rushed to **the theatre** (v. 29). For Gaius and Aristarchus see 20.4. Aristarchus also appears at 27.2, and he is mentioned by Paul at Col. 4.10 and Phlm. 24. In many Greek cities the open-air theatre would be the largest structure with seating, and hence the most suitable site for the meeting of the Assembly of citizens (even at Athens, the specially-constructed meeting place on the Pnyx was abandoned in favour of the theatre of Dionysus after the 4th century BC); the theatre at Ephesus, begun in Claudius' reign (but incorporating parts of an earlier Hellenistic theatre), could, when completed, hold 24,000 people (R. Stillwell [ed.], *Princeton Encyclopaedia of Classical Sites*, p. 309); it is likely that construction was still in progress at the time of the riot narrated in *Acts*. Paul, we are told, **wanted to appear before the assembly** (v. 30). The word translated 'assembly' is *demos* which can either mean 'the people' or can be used as a term in constitutional law for the sovereign body or assembly (see note on 17.5). For the constitutional status of this gathering, see note on v. 32. *NEB* uses 'assembly' as a translation of both *demos* in v. 30 and *ekklesia* in v. 32. He is, however, dissuaded by his friends, who include **some of the dignitaries of the province** (v. 31). The term used for these 'dignitaries' is *Asiarchai*, 'Asiarchs'. There has been a long controversy about the significance of this title, but there can be no doubt that it would only have been held by members of wealthy and aristocratic families. Indeed the geographer Strabo used the holding of the office as proof that Ephesus' neighbour Tralles was well-supplied with wealthy men: 'it is inhabited by as many wealthy men as any city in Asia, and there are always some individuals from the city holding the first positions in the province, whom they call Asiarchs' (Strabo 14, 649). This is a striking example of the author's penchant for presenting Paul as being on intimate terms with the mighty.

In many provinces delegates from the cities met every year as a council (Greek *koinon*) which administered temples and festivals of the provincial (as distinct from civic) worship of the Roman emperors. This council elected a High Priest of the imperial cult who held office for a year. The relation between the title High Priest (*archiereus*) and the titles such as Asiarch, Bithyniarch, Lyciarch, etc., found in inscriptions from several provinces, has long been a matter of debate. One widely held view is that the High Priest for Asia is the Asiarch; another is that ex-High Priests used the title Asiarch for life after their year in office (see J.A.O. Larsen, *Representative Government in Greek and Roman History*, pp. 117-20); but a strong case has been made that, in Lycia at least, there was an annual official called the Lyciarch distinct from the High Priest (S. Jameson, in *ANRW* II [7.2] pp. 843-7).

The confused gathering in the theatre is described as **the assembly** (v. 32; in Greek, *ekklesia*). The use of the term *ekklesia* should mean that this was an official, constitutional meeting of Ephesus' assembly of citizens (cf. v. 41 where the town clerk dismisses the *ekklesia*). Yet the narrative up to this point implies that the silversmiths had marched in a loud demonstration to the theatre, collecting a crowd on the way; and this verse indicates that many of those who had gathered did not know what it was all about and were shouting out inquiries. On the other hand, the theatre was the normal meeting place of the *ekklesia*, and the 'town clerk' (*grammateus*) was its presiding officer (see note on v. 35). The narrative up to this point and a technical use of *ekklesia* could be reconciled in two ways: either a regular meeting had been invaded by the silversmiths (but v. 32 implies that the crowd had been collected by their march); or the arrival of the town clerk to take charge of the meeting conferred on it the status of an *ekklesia*. Or could the author have omitted the technical constitutional preliminaries to calling a meeting of the *ekklesia* either in order to heighten the dramatic effect, or for the sake of brevity? Those attending a hurriedly called meeting of the assembly might not find out what the business was until they got there (though no doubt they could find out in advance if they cared to take the trouble).

Some of the crowd explained the trouble to Alexander, whom the Jews had pushed to the front, and he...attempted to make a defence before the assembly (v. 33), presumably because he and the other Jews are apprehensive about what might be the outcome for their community of the religious agitation which has been stirred up. Like most of the crowd he does not know the precise reason for the disturbance, and has to be informed of it by people from the crowd before he can attempt, unsuccessfully, to make a speech in defence of his community. The Jews presumably wished to dissociate themselves from the Christians, who had angered an element in the native Greek population of the city. Any Jewish leader would have good reason to wish to appease the Gentile population in view of the long-standing resentment felt by Greek cities at the exclusiveness of resident Jews and at the protection they were given by the Roman imperial government. A civic decree of Ephesus, perhaps of 42 BC, declared that no one should be prevented from observing the Sabbath or fined for doing so *after* the Roman governor had granted a Jewish petition about this (Josephus, *Ant.* 14, 262-4); but in 14 BC Marcus Agrippa, then Augustus' co-regent, wrote to the city about theft of the money collected by Jews for the Temple at Jerusalem and the coercion of Jews into appearing in court on the Sabbath (*Ant.* 16, 167-8).

When they recognised that he was a Jew, a single cry arose from them all: for about two hours they kept on shouting 'Great is Diana of the Ephesians!' (v. 34), a response which reveals the hostility aroused among them by the 'atheism' of the Jews, and shows why Alexander needed to make his defence. The same emotions fuelled popular attacks on Christians in cities such as Ephesus in later generations, as recorded in the 'martyr-acts' (e.g. of Polycarp at Smyrna: H. Musurillo, *Acts of the Christian Martyrs*, pp. 9-15). The chanting of this cry in praise of Diana for two hours suggests that, at any rate by this stage, the crowd are motivated by religious fervour rather than the prospect of loss of income.

The town clerk (v. 35) now takes charge. The full title of this elected officer was *grammateus tou demou*, 'Clerk of the People'. Presumably his original function was to keep the minutes of the decisions of the *ekklesia*, but inscriptions and coins show that by this date he had become the chief executive officer of the city and even served as the eponymous magistrate (i.e. the name of that year's Clerk was used to distinguish that year from other years); see Jones, *The Greek City*, pp. 238-9; Sherwin-White (1963) p. 86. He calms the crowd by reassuring them that **all the world knows that our city of Ephesus is temple-warden of the great Diana and of that symbol of her which fell from heaven** (v. 35). 'Temple-warden' translates the Greek *neokoron*, which is applied to the officials responsible for keeping the temple in proper condition; it is related to the verb *neo-korein* 'to tend, keep clean'. The noun came to be used as an honorific description, e.g. at Cyzicus under Gaius (*Sylloge* no. 799, ll. 9-10), and by the time of Hadrian as a title, by cities in the eastern provinces which housed temples of the deified emperors dedicated by the entire province. The greater cities of Asia competed for the honour of being the site of such temples to new emperors. Ephesus acquired her first such temple under Domitian (a temple reconsecrated after his murder to his deified father Vespasian), and a dedication was made to Artemis, the emperor Trajan and 'the temple-warden people of Ephesus' (OGIS no. 481, 1, 3); her second came under Hadrian and in his reign one finds the description 'the *twice* temple-warden city of Ephesus' (OGIS no. 496, 1, 7). In the reign of Caracalla Ephesus acquired a third neokorate and an inscription from the city preserves the emperor's epistle announcing his granting of the Ephesians' request: 'and I have agreed that the city shall be *neokoros* for the third time, but in accordance with my sense of modesty I am offering the *neokory* offered to myself to the goddess most manifest...' (ll. 19-21 of the text as restored by L. Robert, *Revue de Philologie* [1967] pp. 46-57). Hence at that date Ephesus officially became 'temple-warden of Artemis (= Diana)'. Under Elagabalus (218-22) Ephesus was granted a fourth neokorate, and the fact was proudly advertised on the city's coins with the legend: 'alone of all, four times temple-warden' (B.V. Head, *Historia Nummorum*, 2nd edn, p. 577), and a representation of all four temples (reproduced as Fig. 243 in Price and Trell, *Coins and their Cities*). There appears, however, to be no precise parallel from as early as the middle of the 1st century for the phrase used in this verse. **That symbol of her which fell from heaven** translates the two Greek words *tou diopetous*, literally 'the heaven-fallen'. The adjective has no noun with it, but it seems reasonable to assume that it was a meteorite, one of the cult objects associated with the temple of Artemis. Nothing further is known of this object, but the veneration of stones which fell from the sky is known to have been practised in a number of places. Perhaps the best known is the black stone associated with the worship of the sun-god of Emesa, Elagabal, made notorious by the excessive devotion of the emperor Elagabalus.

The Clerk reminds the assembly that there are procedures which can be used to pursue grievances: **Assizes are held, and there are such people as proconsuls; let the parties bring their charges and countercharges** (v. 38); he represents the complaint of Demetrius and his associates as a private quarrel between them and Gaius and Aristarchus, to be settled before the governor's tribunal; presumably Demetrius would complain about interference with the silversmiths' legitimate business, while Gaius and Aristarchus could counter by charging Demetrius and his associates with assault.

The 'assizes' are judicial sessions which were held by Roman governors in their provinces, known in Latin as *conventus iuridici* ('judicial assemblies'). The phrase used here is a technical one for the holding of assizes by a governor (cf. Josephus, *Ant.* 14, 245; Aelius Aristides *Or.* 50, 78, Keil). The Clerk's words sum up very neatly the main function of Roman governors in provinces where there was no important military business to be done. In the larger provinces (and certainly in Asia, about which we have the most information) the governor did not spend his term of office in one place, but went on circuit around the cities of the province holding assizes, much as English judges in criminal cases did until the recent institution of Crown Courts at fixed locations (see G.P. Burton, *JRS* 65 [1975] pp. 92-106 for what is known of the system). Only a minority of cities had the status of an assize-centre, to which litigants in the communities of the surrounding district (known as *conventus* in Latin, but *dioikesis* in Greek) had to travel to go before the governor's tribunal. This status brought both profit (from the crowds of visitors: Dio Chrysostom 35, 15) and prestige to a city (a juristic text ranks cities with assizes below those with the title *metropolis*, but above 'the rest of the cities': *Digest* 27, 1, 6, 2). Hence the competition to acquire this status, illustrated by an epistle of Antoninus Pius from an inscription of Cyrene: 'the people of Berenice asked that assizes should be held in their city also. Now it seemed to me difficult to add to the court-days for, as you in fact know, the proconsul, being in charge of Crete as well as Cyrene, is unable to spend a longer period among you than he does at present' (Reynolds, *JRS*, 68 [1978] p. 114). Ephesus was an assize-centre in the 1st century BC (Josephus, *Ant.* 16, 172), and still had that status 200 years later (Aelius Aristides *Or.* 50, 78, Keil). Ephesus also appears in three lists of the *dioikeseis* of the province of Asia dating from the late Republic, the Augustan period, and the reign of Gaius respectively (C. Habicht, *JRS* 65 [1975] p. 70).

The Clerk next addresses the citizens of Ephesus directly, and invites them to bring any issues they wish to raise to **the statutory assembly** (v. 39); he envisages, no doubt, a formal decree of the *ekklesia* which would probably be directed against an alleged act of impiety towards Artemis, which would certainly concern the whole city (Sherwin-White [1963] p. 83). The Greek term translated 'statutory assembly' is *ennomos ekklesia*; a very similar phrase, *nomimos ekklesia*, does occur in an inscription from Ephesus (E. L. Hicks, *Ancient Greek Inscriptions in the British Museum* III [2] no. 481, ll. 54 and 339-40). It presumably referred to regularly scheduled meetings prescribed by law (forty such meetings were scheduled each year in classical Athens: [Aristotle] *Ath. Pol.* 43, 3), in contrast to extraordinary meetings convened by the Council or the Clerk. The commentators cite an assertion by St. John Chrysostom (*Homilies on Acts* 42,

2) that there were three such *ekklesiai* at Ephesus each month, and Sherwin-White (1963, p. 87) suggested that the phrase 'holy and lawful assembly' in an inscription was used to distinguish one of these meetings from the other two. One may, however, be sceptical about what evidence, if any, Chrysostom, who was writing at a period when city assemblies had long been defunct, had for this assertion.

As the events are narrated in *Acts*, the present gathering had not begun as even an extraordinary *ekklesia*, but as a demonstration to which the terms 'riot' and 'uproar' are applied (v. 40). Nevertheless it is here implied that it was an *ekklesia* and is described as such by the author when the Clerk dissolves it at the end of v. 40 (see note on v. 32).

The Clerk concludes with a warning: **We...run the risk of being charged with riot** (v. 40). This must refer to the reaction of the proconsul (and possibly the emperor) to news of the event; for the extreme anxiety of the Roman authorities about disturbances in the Greek cities, see notes on vv. 23 and 25, and Introduction pp. 18-20. The clerk envisages actions which would affect the civic institutions of Ephesus ('*We* run the risk...'); soon after AD 100 the *ekklesia* of the city of Prusa was forbidden to meet by the proconsul of Bithynia-Pontus (Dio Chrysostom *Or.* 48). The inscribed edict from Ephesus about the bakers cited in the note to v. 23 shows how a proconsul could react to behaviour such as theirs: 'Those charged with taking part in such disturbances should already have paid the penalty. But, since one must count the interest of the city as more important than retaliation against these men, I have considered it necessary to bring them to their senses by an edict. Wherefore I forbid the bakers to assemble as a club or to take the lead in insolence; instead I order them to obey completely those made responsible for the public interest and to supply the city without fail with the necessary output of bread. Whenever any of them may be caught hereafter either assembling contrary to the ban or starting some hubbub and riot, he shall be charged and be punished with the appropriate retaliation' (ll. 3-11 of the text cited in the note to v. 23).

Chapter 20

Paul leaves Ephesus, and travels through Greece and Macedonia; he sails down the coast of Asia Minor to Miletus; he summons the elders of the church in Ephesus, and tells them of his decision to go to Jerusalem.

Paul travels (presumably by sea) to Macedonia, and from there **came into Greece** (v. 2); the Greek name for the country, *Hellas*, is used, but presumably the Roman province of Achaia is meant.

Paul's companions on the journey from Macedonia are listed in v. 4.

Sopater may be the Sosipater of Rom. 16.21. **Aristarchus** we have met at 19.29; here we are given the additional information that he is from Thessalonica, like **Secundus** (otherwise unknown). If **Gaius** is really, as most manuscripts say, from Derbe, he cannot be the Gaius of 19.29, who is a Macedonian (unless that adjective is in the singular, which is the reading of some manuscripts, so that it only applies to Aristarchus); if, however, with *NEB* we adopt the reading **Doberian** instead, the difficulty is solved, since Doberus was in Macedonia, not far from Philippi. **Timothy** we last left at 19.22. A **Tychicus** appears also at Col. 4.7, Eph. 6.21, Tit. 3.12, 2 Tim. 4.12. **Trophimus** reappears at 21.29, and perhaps also at 2 Tim. 4.20. This group travels directly to Troas, while another group (including the 'we' which returns in v. 6) only sails for Troas after the Passover. It is not made clear which group includes Paul.

In introducing the episode covered in vv. 7-12 (the rescue by Paul of a young man apparently dead), the author refers in passing to a meeting for **the breaking of bread** (v. 7). Whatever this meeting involved, it does not look like a regular meal, and is probably a reference which only Christian readers would understand (see notes to 2.42).

At v. 13, a group including the 'we' sails from Troas to Assos, clearly this time without Paul, who travels overland. The journey by land is shorter than by sea, and, if the winds were not favourable, probably quicker. In either case the distance is not far. From Assos they sail down the coast, calling at **Mytilene, Chios,** and **Samos,** until they reach **Miletus** (v. 16), an itinerary which illustrates the normal practice of merchant ships, passing from port to port in short hops, and no doubt unloading and taking on goods and passengers at each port. Miletus is not far from Ephesus, from which he summons **the elders of the congregation** (v. 17). We are not told why he does not go to Ephesus himself. The statement that he wished **to avoid having to spend time in the province of Asia** (v. 16) is a restatement of his decision, rather than an explanation.

The address to the elders of Ephesus has implications for our understanding of the ending of *Acts*. It reads like a speech of farewell. Paul himself is made to say: **I know that none of you will see my face again** (v. 25). This phrase is then taken up by the narrator: **What distressed them most was his saying that they would never see his face again** (v. 38). It is difficult to believe that the author could have written these words at a time when Paul was still alive. If so, it is not possible that *Acts* was completed before Paul's death.

Chapter 21

Paul sails to Caesarea and stays with Philip; he travels to Jerusalem, and reports to James and the elders; some Jews from Asia accuse him of profaning the temple, and he is arrested by the Romans.

The ship in which Paul is sailing makes its way from port to port in short hops as far as Patara, on the south-western tip of Asia Minor. It would probably be a vessel of the kind described by the younger Pliny as 'coastal vessels' (*Epistles* 10, 15) which would not venture to cross the open sea (see L. Casson, *The Ancient Mariners*, pp. 114-15). The ship they pick up at Patara sails directly to Tyre and, since they pass Cyprus **leaving it to port** (v. 3; the Greek says, more helpfully, 'on the left'), must have cut across the open sea instead of following the mainland coast east and then south, saving a considerable amount of time. The ship puts in to Tyre **to unload her cargo** (v. 3). There were no purpose-built passenger ships in antiquity. Those wishing to travel by sea (even on official business: see 27.6) would have to take passage on a merchant ship. Most passengers would pass the voyage camping on the deck, though the very rich and powerful might take the captain's cabin; they would be responsible for providing their own food, though they do seem to have been supplied with water (for the carriage of passengers and freight, and the construction and management of larger merchant ships in the Roman period, see Casson, op. cit., pp. 191-7).

Tyre (v. 3) was one of the four major trading cities of the Phoenicians, which was resettled by Alexander after he sacked the city in 332 (Jones, *Cities*, pp. 237-9). The ship remains there seven days, presumably to unload one cargo and pick up another. In Tyre they stayed with **the disciples** (v. 4) who, **warned by the Spirit, urged Paul to abandon his visit to Jerusalem** (v. 4). Like the address to the elders of Ephesus (20.18-35), and the warning of Abagus later (v. 11), the purpose of this report is to prepare for momentous events later in Jerusalem and then Rome; we are approaching some sort of climax. The disciples are presumably converts made in the mission reported in 11.19.

The ship's next port of call is **Ptolemais** (v. 7), the ancient town of Akka (later Acre, capital of the crusader kingdom after 1187; now Akko in Israel), renamed after the dynastic name of the Ptolemies of Egypt. For the port where Paul and his companions disembark, **Caesarea** (v. 8), see note on 10.1. **Philip the evangelist, who was one of the Seven** (v. 8) was last recorded reaching Caesarea at 8.40. He is perhaps called 'the evangelist' (in the sense 'missionary', not the modern sense of 'author of a gospel') and 'one of the Seven' (see 6.3-5) to distinguish him from Philip who was one of the twelve apostles. His **four unmarried daughters, who possessed the gift of prophecy** (v. 9) reappear later in the historical tradition as giving information to Papias, one of the sources used by Eusebius (*Ecclesiastical History* 3, 39, 9; there may however have been some confusion in the reports used by Eusebius, who seems to identify Philip with the apostle). Next the prophet **Agabus** (see 11.28) **arrived from Judaea** (v. 10), or, as more literally translated by *RSV*, **came down from Judaea**. 'Judaea' is used in the narrower sense of the hill country around Jerusalem (hence 'came down'), between Samaria and Idumaea, the original core of Jewish settlement before territorial expansion under the Hasmoneans around 100 BC (see W.D. Davies and L. Finkelstein, *The Cambridge History of Judaism* vol. 2, ch. 1). Although it lay in the Roman province of Judaea, Caesarea, as a pagan city on the coast, did not count as part of Judaea in the narrower sense.

Despite Agabus' warnings, Paul travels up to Jerusalem where he meets James (see 15.13) and **all the elders** (v. 18). The question of Gentile converts appears to have been raised again (v. 21); the ruling of chapter 15 is reiterated (v. 25); and Paul is asked to demonstrate that he himself is still a practising Jew by paying the expenses of four men (presumably Jewish Christians) who have undertaken what appears to be a Nazirite vow (vv. 23-4; see note on 18.18).

But before he can perform this public act to demonstrate his continued acceptance of the Jewish law, trouble breaks out when **the Jews from the province of Asia saw him in the temple** (v. 27). Presumably they are pilgrims from Ephesus, because they recognise **Trophimus the Ephesian** (v. 29) and, believing that Paul has brought Trophimus, a Gentile, into the temple, they make the accusation that **he has brought Gentiles into the temple and profaned this holy place** (v. 28). Josephus records repeated riots provoked by supposed profanation of the temple between AD 6 and 66: see the narrative in Schürer[2] I, pp. 382-6 and 455-70. After Herod's reconstruction there was a huge courtyard on the Temple mount, surrounded by colonnades, which Gentiles were free to enter; within this there was a much smaller area around the actual Temple structure which Jews alone could enter. In Josephus' *Jewish War* (6, 124-6; cf. 5, 193-4) Titus Caesar is made to say that Rome had allowed the execution even of Roman citizens who violated the ban on Gentiles entering this inner court. Inscriptions in Greek and Latin were put up warning Gentiles not to do so, and two of these (in Greek) have been recovered in modern times. One can be translated thus: 'No foreigner is to pass within the railing and enclosure around the temple; whosoever may be caught will be responsible to himself for the fact that death is the result' (OGIS no. 598; cf. *Supplementum Epigraphicum Graecum* VIII, no. 169; for a photograph see A. Deissman, *Light from the Ancient East*, p. 80, Fig. 9).

The ensuing riot, in the course of which Paul is seized and threatened with death (vv. 30-1) provokes the intervention of **the officer commanding the cohort** (v. 31) accompanied by **a force of soldiers with their centurions** (v. 32), who save Paul by arresting him. In Greek 'the officer' is a *chiliarchos* (literally = commander of a thousand) and 'cohort' translates *speira*. The word *speira* (cf. note on 10.1) had been used as the name of a unit of the army of the Ptolemies, and then by Greek authors for two different Latin terms, *manipulus* (a unit obsolete by the 1st century) and *cohors*. A 'cohort' was originally one of the ten units into which a Roman legion was divided, but the term came also to be used for an independent unit of infantry (500 or 1,000 strong) recruited from non-Romans ('auxiliaries'). Since no legions were stationed in Judaea before AD 66, it is a unit of the second kind which is stationed in Jerusalem and is referred to here. The normal Latin title for the commander of such a unit was *praefectus*, and the normal Greek equivalent for this was *eparchos* (see H.J. Mason, *Greek Terms for Roman Institutions*, pp. 138-40). *Chiliarchos* (or *-es*), on the other hand, was used as the equivalent of the Latin title *tribunus militum*, 'tribune of the soldiers' (Mason, pp. 99-100). There were six such 'tribunes' serving as junior officers in each legion, but the title was also held by the commanders of some auxiliary cohorts, those composed of Roman citizens and those which were a thousand strong (*milliaria*) rather than five hundred strong (*quingenaria*), as was more usual (G.R. Watson, *The Roman Soldier*, pp. 15-16, 25; P.A. Holder, *The Auxilia from Augustus to Trajan*, pp. 77 and 79). Hence it has been suggested that this was either a cohort of Roman citizens (cf. note on 10.1; Sherwin-White [1963] p. 155, n. 2) or a cohort of a thousand (BC IV, p. 275). But these suggestions depend on the author of *Acts* being aware of the distinction between *eparchos* and *chiliarchos* in this context. Each of the **centurions** (v. 32; cf. note on 10.1) would be in command of one of the centuries into which the cohort was divided. The plural implies that Lysias (see 23.26) brought with him at least two centuries. Josephus reports that there was a cohort permanently stationed in the Antonia (see note on v. 34) until 66 (*War* 5, 244).

The soldiers take Paul to **the barracks** (v. 34) by way of **the steps** (v. 35). The Greek word translated 'barracks' is *parembole* (literally = encampment) and must refer to the tower built by Herod I to the north-west of the Temple court and named *Antonia* after Marcus Antonius (Josephus, *War* 1, 401; 5, 238-45); it was linked to the colonnades around the outer court of the Temple precinct by the **steps** (Josephus, *War* 5, 243).

Before entering the barracks Paul speaks to **the commandant** (v. 37; this is the *chiliarchos* in command of the cohort). The commandant is surprised at being addressed in Greek: **So you speak Greek, do you?** (v. 37). The implication of the question is that it would be surprising if an ordinary Palestinian Jew could speak Greek, and in the next verse it is suggested that the speaker is likely to be a Jew of the Diaspora (which Paul in fact was). Yet it is quite clear that a Diaspora Jew (whether Paul or the Egyptian of v. 38) would normally be Greek speaking (see notes on 2.9-11 and 6.1). Moreover, other evidence suggests that the ability to speak Greek was, at least in Jerusalem, more widespread than this verse would suggest: see T. Rajak, *Josephus* chapter 2; J.N. Sevenster, *Do you know Greek?* (with the review by D.M. Lewis in *J. Theol. Stud.* 20. p. 583ff.). The dichotomy in the Christian church between 'Hellenists' and 'Hebrews' (6.1) does suggest some sort of division which was, at least partly, on linguistic lines. The commandant then reveals that he has assumed that Paul was **the Egyptian who started a revolt some time ago and led a force of four thousand terrorists out into the wilds** (v. 38). Josephus (*Ant.* 20, 169-71; *War* 2, 261-3) describes the activities in AD 54 of a 'false prophet' from Egypt, who won support by a promise that the walls of Jerusalem would collapse at his command, and who disappeared when his followers were routed by soldiers sent out by the governor Felix (Schürer[2] I, p. 464; Smallwood, *The Jews under Roman Rule*, pp. 274-5). The manuscripts of Josephus *War* 2, 261 give the number of his followers as 30,000. The figure in *Acts* is more plausible, and it has been suggested that in the text of Josephus an original capital delta (= 4) has been corrupted into capital lambda (= 30) (BC IV, p. 277). 'Terrorists' is a translation of the Greek word *sikarioi*, itself a transliteration of the Latin term *sicarii* (literally = dagger-men); this word was used, in Roman legislation, along with *veneficii* (= poisoners), to refer to murderers. Josephus uses the term to describe individual Jews who carried out acts of political murder in the years before the revolt of AD 66, because the method they used was to stab unsuspecting victims by mingling with the crowds at the great religious festivals (*War* 2, 254-7; *Ant.* 20, 185-7). Later he used the word to refer to the group of Jewish rebels who withdrew to the fortress of Masada (*War* 7, 252-8). Josephus actually says that the Egyptian led his followers *out* of the wilderness to the Mount of Olives, not *into* it. Distinct from him, and from the *sicarii*, were the unnamed 'deceivers and charlatans' who led their dupes out into the wilderness.

Paul replied, 'I am a Jew, a Tarsian from Cilicia, a citizen of no mean city' (v. 39), which distinguishes him from the Egyptian Jew, explains his ability to speak Greek, and (perhaps) indicates that he is not one of the Jerusalem rabble (since he enjoys citizen status of a perfectly respectable Greek city). In many Greek cities (and especially in Alexandria) the citizens of Greek ancestry objected to Jews acquiring full citizenship (Schürer[2] III [1] pp. 126-32). At least some of Paul's family, however, seem to be resident in Jerusalem (23.16).

With the commandant's permission, Paul addresses the crowd **in the Jewish language** (v. 40). In the original Greek he is said to speak 'in Hebrew', but the language used is probably Aramaic, which was the *lingua franca* of Palestine and the surrounding area (though there is evidence of a limited survival of Hebrew, which would, of course, still be used in the Temple). What Paul is presumably trying to do is to reassure the crowd of his complete Jewishness (which was also the point of the elders' advice to him: vv. 23-4). For Hebrew and Aramaic in Palestine, see Schürer[2] II, pp. 20-8; T. Rajak, *Josephus*, pp. 230-2.

Chapter 22

Paul's words fail to satisfy the crowd; the Romans are about to give him a flogging, but stop when he reveals his Roman citizenship.

Paul begins his speech by asserting **I am a true-born Jew** (v. 3; perhaps an over-translation of the Greek, which says simply 'I am a Jew'). He then makes the claim that he is not just a Jew, but one brought up in the most conservative traditions of Judaism: **I was brought up in this city, and as a pupil of Gamaliel I was thoroughly trained in every point of our ancestral law** (v. 3; for Gamaliel, see note on 5.34). In other words, though he was born in Tarsus, he is not one of those Diaspora Jews who are dangerously tainted with Hellenism. He then narrates his persecution of the Christians, and his conversion on the way to Damascus. Paul stresses that Ananias, who received him in Damascus after his conversion (9.10-19) was **a devout observer of the Law and well spoken of by all the Jews of that place** (v. 12). Finally, his mission to the Gentiles is the result of a direct command from God delivered while **praying in the temple** (v. 17). In short, Paul is as devout and traditional a Jew as they are; only direct intervention from God has made him a Christian, and sent him to preach to the Gentiles.

The crowd are not at all impressed by this speech, and, seeing the disorder, the commandant **gave instructions to examine him by flogging, and find out what reason there was for such an outcry against him** (v. 24). Sherwin-White (1963, pp. 27-8) describes this as an example of a 'cautionary beating', but the commandant is depicted here as using it as a form of torture to obtain evidence (the Greek, but not the English translation, makes it clear that the flogging is to be given *in order that* he might find out what Paul has said to annoy the crowd). The evidence of slaves was valid in Roman courts only if given under torture, but free men should in theory have been immune from torture as witnesses (P. Garnsey, *Social Status and Legal Privilege in the Roman Empire*, pp. 143-5 and 213-5).

Paul protests that he is a Roman citizen, in much the same terms (and to the same effect) as he and Silas had done in Philippi (see note on 16.37): **Can you legally flog a man who is a Roman citizen, and moreover has not been found guilty?** (v. 25). The commandant, on hearing this, is surprised, and says: **It cost me a large sum to acquire this citizenship** (v. 28). He was therefore, unlike Paul (v. 28), not a citizen by birth; his name,

Claudius Lysias (see 23.26), reveals that he was a Greek named Lysias
who had received citizenship through an individual grant from an emperor,
whose clan-name (*gentilicium*), Claudius, he had then taken, as was common practice among the newly-enfranchised. That could only have been
the reigning emperor, Nero Claudius Caesar, or, more probably, Nero's
predecessor, Tiberius Claudius Caesar. The 'large sum' can only have been
a bribe paid to one of the imperial freedmen who had such great influence
over Claudius, in order to secure the grant; see the (perhaps exaggerated)
account of the historian Cassius Dio (60, 17, 5f.): 'Many sought citizenship
from the emperor himself, and many bought it...from his freedmen. For
this reason, though it was sold at first for large sums, it later became so
cheapened...that the saying was that you could become a citizen by giving
pieces of glass'. See also Sherwin-White (1963) pp. 154-6.

  Paul is released, a meeting of **the chief priests and the entire Council**
(v. 30) is called, and Paul is taken to appear before them. For this Council
(the *Sanhedrin*) see notes on 5.21; for the high-priests see notes on 4.6.

Chapter 23

Paul's appearance before the Council is the cause of a riot; the comman-
dant is informed of a conspiracy to murder Paul, and has him transferred
to Caesarea.

When Paul attempts to defend himself **the High Priest Ananias ordered**
his attendants to strike him on the mouth (v. 2). Ananias son of Nede-
baios was High Priest from around 47 to 58, and was eventually assassinated after the outbreak of the revolt in 66 (Josephus, *War* 2, 441). If *Acts*
was composed after 66, then Paul's retort, **God will strike you, you white-**
washed wall! (v. 3), could be a prediction 'after the event', or words
which seemed natural at the time but were seen as significant in the light of
their apparent fulfilment. It is not at all clear why Paul calls Ananias a
whitewashed wall. Jesus does compare the lawyers and Pharisees to
'tombs covered with whitewash' (Matt. 23.27), but his point is the contrast
between external appearance and internal reality, which a wall will not
convey. Perhaps there is a reference to the building painted with whitewash in *Ezekiel* (13.14), which God will lay low. The author stresses that
Paul did not know it was the High Priest he was addressing (v. 4).

  The author has already introduced us to the disagreements between
Pharisees and Sadducees (see 4.1-2 and 5.34, and notes to these passages).
Paul plays on these divisions, announcing that he is **a Pharisee born and**
bred (v. 6), and that the real issue at stake was **the resurrection of the**
dead (v. 6) which the Sadducees denied. Again, the disorder this provokes

is so great that Paul has to be rescued by Roman soldiers.

A plot is formed to murder Paul on the way to another appearance before the Council next day; but **the son of Paul's sister** (v. 16) hears of the plan, and passes the information on first to Paul and then to the commandant. This is the first we hear of any family of Paul, and the first indication that his family is resident in Jerusalem. Otherwise, we might have assumed that Paul was simply a visitor, or perhaps a student, in Jerusalem when he became involved with the Christians.

The commandant makes the decision to send Paul to Caesarea with an escort of **two hundred infantry...together with seventy cavalrymen and two hundred light-armed troops** (v. 23). The usual deduction made from the presence of cavalry along with the 200 infantrymen is that the cohort under Lysias' command was one of mixed infantry and cavalry (called a *cohors equitata* in Latin): see BC IV, p. 275. But there was an *ala* of cavalry stationed in Judaea in the time of the procurators (Josephus *War* 2, 236; *Ant.* 20, 122); it had been inherited, along with five infantry cohorts, from Agrippa I, and was recruited from the local Gentiles of Sebaste. It could have been based at Jerusalem at this date. 'Light-armed troops' is a translation of Greek *dexiolaboi* (in some manuscripts *dexioboloi*); since the term is not found again for five centuries, it is wholly unclear what kind of troops the author of *Acts* thought he meant (Schürer[2] I, p. 366).

Paul is to be taken to **Felix the governor** (v. 24). The author of *Acts* uses the general Greek word for governor, *hegemon* (= leader), instead of the more precise *epitropos* (= Latin *procurator*). Felix was appointed to this post by Claudius about AD 52 (Josephus, *War* 2, 247; *Ant.* 20, 137; Schürer[2] I, p. 460, n. 17). This man was himself a freedman of Claudius and the brother of the even more influential freedman Pallas; at this period procurators, even when governors of small provinces, were still regarded so much as the emperor's personal agents that it was still possible for imperial freedmen to hold positions of command; after Nero's death such an appointment would have been unthinkable. Suetonius (*Claudius* 28) describes Felix as the husband of three 'queens', and one of these was a Jewess, Drusilla, the daughter of King Agrippa I (see 24.24), whom he induced to leave her first husband (during his governorship: Josephus *Ant.* 20, 141-3; Josephus tells us that the go-between Felix used to lure Drusilla away from her husband, Azizus king of Emesa, was the Cypriot Jewish magician Atomos: see note on 13.8).

And he wrote a letter (v. 25), but the text given in *Acts*, like other letters (and speeches) in classical histories, was composed by the author. No plausible way can be suggested for him to have obtained access to any such actual letter written by Lysias, and no proper archives of such correspondence were maintained in Roman provinces. We are, however, given the commandant's name, **Claudius Lysias** (v. 26; see note on 22.28).

The full escort takes Paul as far as **Antipatris** (v. 31), a new (and pagan) city built on the coastal plain (some 25 miles south of Caesarea) by Herod I, and named after his father (Jones, *Cities*, p. 275; Schürer² II, pp. 167-8). The infantry leave at this point because on the coastal plain a cavalry escort alone would be quite satisfactory.

The governor, on receiving Paul and the covering letter, first asks **what province he was from** (v. 34). Sherwin-White (1963, pp. 28-31) argued that in the 1st century AD the normal practice was for a criminal charge to be tried by the governor of the province in which the alleged crime had been committed, but that the practice had begun to emerge of sending an accused man who came from another province to be tried by the governor of that province, in exceptional circumstances. Felix's question implies an awareness of this possibility but, on learning that Paul came from Cilicia, he decided not to trouble the governor of Syria, who in the mid-50s was probably in charge of Cilicia (Sherwin-White [1963] pp. 55-7).

Until his accusers arrive, Paul is kept in the governor's **headquarters in Herod's palace** (v. 35), or more literally with *RSV*, **in Herod's praetorium**. The Latin word *praetorium* referred to the headquarters of a Roman commander inside a military camp, and also to any permanent residence available to a Roman governor in his civilian capacity. The Roman state did not normally build such residences, but it did appropriate royal palaces in territories it annexed, as at Syracuse (Cicero 2 *Verr.* 5. 80) and in Jerusalem (Matt. 27.27; Mark 15.16; John 18.33; 19.9). The palace must have been built by Herod I, the founder of Caesarea (Schürer² I, p. 361; see also note to 24.27).

Chapter 24

Paul's opponents present their case, and he defends himself; though no fault is found with him, he remains in prison.

Paul's examination by Felix begins when **the High Priest Ananias came down accompanied by some of the elders and an advocate named Tertullus** (v. 1). For Ananias see note on 23.2. The word translated 'advocate' is the Greek *rhetor* (= orator). Rhetoric was an important element in ancient education. It was valued, not just as a valuable tool for persuasion in trials or political assemblies, but as an art in its own right. A governor or an emperor would expect from anyone before them not just a competent exposition, but also a high degree of artistry (G.W. Bowersock, *Greek Sophists in the Roman Empire* ch. 4). Ananias is therefore employing an expert to make his case. Tertullus has an ordinary Roman name, but, as usual, no inferences about his status can be drawn from it; the use of the

1st person plural, especially in the account of Paul's arrest, suggests, if anything, that he is a Jew.

Tertullus' speech (vv. 2-8) begins, as normal, with compliments to the governor, stressing the **unbroken peace** (v. 3) which the province allegedly enjoys (and which Paul is accused of threatening). He represents Paul as a **fomenter of discord** (v. 5), a political charge, namely incitement to riot; but if the evidence for the charge was mostly of a theological nature, then the procurator's bafflement later would be explained (Sherwin-White [1963] p. 51). When Tertullus claims that Paul is a leader of **the sect of the Nazarenes** (v. 5) he uses the same word, *hairesis*, as was used earlier of the Sadducees (5.17 and see note on 4.1). He closes with the claim that Paul was arrested for attempting to profane the Temple, and his assertions are supported by witnesses (v. 9).

Paul's defence begins, like Tertullus' speech, with a compliment to the governor, this time for **justice** (v. 10). He denies that he has caused trouble in Jerusalem (v. 12), and disarms Tertullus' insinuation that he is the leader of some new, and potentially disruptive *hairesis* by admitting openly that he is **a follower of the new way (the 'sect' they speak of) and it is in that manner that I worship the God of our fathers** (v. 14). 'The way' (Greek *he hodos*) is a common term in *Acts* for Christianity (e.g. 9.2, 19.9, 19.23, 22.4).

The origins of the usage are unclear, but it may have parallels in rabbinical texts. Occasionally it appears as 'the way of the Lord' (18.25), or 'the way of God' (18.26). Compare such Septuagint expressions as 'the ways of the Gentiles' (Jer. 10.2), and the two ways in the *Didache* 1: 'there are two ways, one of life, and one of death', (a passage which may be derived from a pre-Christian Jewish source). Here Paul is trying to suggest that Christianity is just another form of traditional Judaism, and nothing new or disturbing. In the time of the persecutions one of the main objections of Roman authorities to Christians (usually of Gentile ancestry) was that they refused to worship the gods of *their* ancestors; as Gibbon put it, in Roman eyes 'the Jews were a people which followed, the Christians a sect which deserted, the Religion of their Fathers'.

His challenge to his accusers: **some Jews from the province of Asia were there** (sc. in the Temple when the alleged attempt at profanation took place) **and if they had any charge against me it is they who ought to have been in court to state it** (v. 19) is a sound point under Roman law (Sherwin-White [1963] p. 52).

After Paul's speech, Felix **adjourned the hearing** (v. 22) pending the arrival of Lysias (of whom in fact we hear nothing further). We are told that Felix was **well informed about the Christian movement** (v. 22) or more literally with *RSV*, about **the Way**, using the same term as Paul had in v. 14; we must assume that the author intends us to believe that such knowledge would predispose him in Paul's favour, but we are not told how he got it. For **Drusilla** (v. 24) see note on 23.24.

Felix keeps Paul in custody, according to *Acts* because he **had hopes of a bribe** (v. 26), which is plausible enough. The date at which **when two years had passed Felix was succeeded by Porcius Festus** (v. 27) has been a matter of dispute among scholars. The dispute is linked to the interpretation of the 'when' clause; were the 'two years' the length of Felix's term or of Paul's period of detention? The latter is obviously the more natural interpretation, and the former could only be adopted if it were certain that Felix's recall took place early in Nero's reign (at the end of 54 or in 55). However, the case for this early date is demolished in Schürer² I, p. 465, n. 42. Felix's recall probably took place in AD 60 (possibly 59). Festus is only known (outside *Acts*) from Josephus (*War* 2, 271; *Ant.* 20, 182); he remained procurator until 62.

Felix had good reasons, namely fear of prosecution for misgovernment, for **wishing to curry favour with the Jews** (v. 27). In the event a prosecution was launched by the Jews of Caesarea alone, but Felix was acquitted because of the influence his brother Pallas had with Nero (Josephus. *Ant.* 20, 182). At any rate, whatever his motives, he **left Paul in custody** (v. 27). In three of his epistles, Paul describes himself as being 'in bonds' (*Philippians*, *Colossians*, and *Philemon*). Many scholars have held that these were written while he was awaiting trial at Rome (see 28.16 and 30) because in Philippians he refers to his bonds being known 'in the whole *praetorium*', and sends the greetings of 'those in Caesar's household' (Phil. 1.13; 4.22); these words are taken to refer to the several thousand members of the emperor's Praetorian Guard, and to the enormous numbers of slaves and freedmen in the imperial palace. However, since *praetorium* is used elsewhere in the New Testament only in reference to the governor's residences at Caesarea and Jerusalem, it is likely that Paul was referring to 'Herod's *praetorium*' where he was detained at Caesarea (see note on 23.35); in that case 'those from Caesar's household' would be the imperial freedmen and slaves who assisted the procurator in the financial administration of Judaea (equestrian procurators, unlike senatorial proconsuls and legates, were in charge of finance as well as law and order: Schürer² I, p. 359), and who would have been based in the *praetorium* at Caesarea.

Chapter 25

Festus hears the charges against Paul, and suggests returning him to Jerusalem for trial; Paul appeals to Caesar, and Festus agrees to send him to Rome; Festus asks the advice of Agrippa.

Festus, immediately on appointment, takes steps to bring Paul's case to a conclusion. He holds a new hearing in Caesarea, and when, presumably in order to **ingratiate himself with the Jews** (v. 9) and create a good impression at the beginning of his tenure of office, he seems inclined to accede to the request of Paul's accusers to move the trial to Jerusalem, Paul protests: **I am now standing before the Emperor's tribunal, and that is where I must be tried** (v. 10). In theory the procurator was *not* exercising a jurisdiction delegated by the emperor, but, as Sherwin-White (1963) observes (pp. 66-7) 'a provincial might well regard the governor's tribunal as the tribunal of the Princeps'.

Finally, Paul declares: **I appeal to Caesar!** (v. 11). Festus **after conferring with his advisers, replied 'You have appealed to Caesar: to Caesar you shall go'** (v. 12). It was the universal practice of Roman officials, when they acted as judges, to summon a group of advisers (*consilium*), chosen by themselves, and, after hearing the case, to discuss it in private with these advisers before delivering a judgement (in public). See J. Crook, *Consilium Principis*, ch. 1; *Law and Life of Rome*, pp. 88-9; Sherwin-White (1963) pp. 17-21.

These two verses (11 and 12) present some of the most contentious problems of interpretation in *Acts*. It is difficult to assess how far the author of *Acts* has given an accurate account of an 'appeal to Caesar', because his account of this incident is itself one of the main pieces of evidence upon which any reconstruction of the Roman law of appeal in the 1st century has to be based.

The conventional account of the Roman law of appeal is given by A.H.M. Jones (*Studies in Roman Government and Law* ch. 4; *The Criminal Courts of the Roman Republic and Principate*, pp. 101-2, where Jones comments that 'one is led to suspect that neither Paul nor his biographer understood the legal position') and by Sherwin-White (1963, pp. 57-70). This account was challenged by P. Garnsey (*JRS* vol. 56 [1966] pp. 167-89; *Social Status and Legal Privilege in the Roman Empire*, pp. 71-9). The inadequacy of our evidence for establishing what the legal basis for an 'appeal to Caesar' was has been stressed by F. Millar (*The Emperor in the Roman World*, pp. 507-16): cf. his remarks on Paul's case, 'no adequate criterion exists for checking the historicity of the narrative of *Acts*; as it stands, it will tell us nothing about any precise rules of Roman law which may have been applicable in this area, but a lot about the power of the name of Caesar in the minds both of his subjects and of his appointees' (op. cit. p. 511).

The conventional account is that the right of *provocatio* which all Roman citizens had (in theory) enjoyed under the Republic was transformed under the rule of the emperors into a right of *appellatio*. *Provocatio* had been to the Roman People in their voting assemblies, but *appellatio* was 'to Caesar'. *Provocatio* would be used by a citizen against the imposition by any Roman magistrate of a sentence of execution or flogging or an order for torture: 'any holder of *imperium* or power is liable under the Julian law about public violence who executes or flogs...a Roman citizen in violation of *provocatio*' (Ulpian, *Digest* 48, 6, 7). The jurist Paul referred to the transformation of the right: 'under the Julian law on public violence anyone endowed with any power who has executed, ordered to be executed, tortured, flogged...a Roman citizen who appeals, formerly to the people, now to the emperor, is condemned' (*Sententiae Pauli* 5, 26, 1).

Garnsey criticised Jones for suggesting that Paul's case represented an earlier form of 'appeal to Caesar' which took place before sentence, whereas all the Roman legal authorities (of the 3rd century) depict appeal as only being possible after sentence. He said that 'if Paul's appeal is "*provocatio*-before-trial" in the sense assumed by Jones and Sherwin-White, there is no parallel which is of any use, and consequently the case has to be explained in the light of itself' (*Social Status and Legal Privilege in the Roman Empire*, p. 75, n. 4). Jones subsequently changed his view: 'Paul's *provocatio* was irregular; he had not been condemned, and *provocatio* (and *appellatio*) could only be made after condemnation.... He (Festus) apparently regularised the position by deeming Paul to have been condemned; at any rate Paul went to Rome in chains under military escort' (*Criminal Courts of the Roman Republic and Principate*, p. 102).

It is difficult to use the evidence of the Roman citizen's right of 'appeal to Caesar' to explain the narrative in *Acts*, for three reasons: (1) Paul's status as a Roman citizen is nowhere mentioned; (2) Paul acts *before* Festus has imposed any sentence; (3) Festus appears to be granting a request which he was free to reject, rather than respecting a right which a governor could be prosecuted for disregarding (see note on 25.25). The narrative can better be explained in terms of political 'manoeuvering' rather than of exercising legal rights. Paul, anxious to avoid a trial in Jerusalem, invoked the name of Caesar to bring pressure to bear on Festus: 'To sacrifice me to appease my Jewish enemies might lead you into political difficulties later at Rome, if it becomes known that I had asked to have the matter referred to the emperor.' Festus, torn between this pressure and his wish to keep on the right side of the Jewish leaders, was surely glad to have Paul off his hands.

Shortly afterwards **King Agrippa and Bernice arrived at Caesarea on a courtesy visit to Festus** (v. 13); for similar state visits described by Josephus, see *War* 2, 309; 481. Agrippa II (son of Agrippa I: see ch. 12) had been at Rome when his father died in 44, and Claudius was persuaded that, at the age of 17, he was too young to succeed his father (Schürer[2] I, pp. 453-4). However, around 50 he had been appointed king over the territories in the Lebanon previously ruled by his uncle (and brother-in-law)

Herod of Chalcis (Schürer[2] I, pp. 571-2), and he also took over from his uncle the function of choosing the High Priests at Jerusalem; in 53 he was given, in exchange for Chalcis, more extensive territories to the north-east of the province of Judaea. He failed to prevent the revolt at Jerusalem in 66, remained Rome's ally, and kept his dominions until his death in the last decade of the 1st century (Schürer[2] I, pp. 471-83).

Bernice (the correct Macedonian form of the name was Berenice) was the eldest of Agrippa's three sisters. Her first husband had been her uncle Herod of Chalcis, but after his death in 48 she appears as her brother's virtual co-regent (despite a second, short-lived, marriage to Polemon, king in Cilicia, around AD 64-6). This association led to the charge of incest brought by the satirist Juvenal (6, 156-60; cf. Josephus *Ant.* 20, 145). Berenice became most notorious in subsequent history (and especially in drama and opera) as the mistress of the future emperor Titus Caesar in the 70s (Schürer[2] I, pp. 474 and 479).

Festus discusses Paul's case with Agrippa and Berenice. He says that he refused demands for his condemnation because: **It is not Roman practice to hand over any accused man before he is confronted with his accusers and given an opportunity of answering the charge** (v. 16), which is an accurate statement of standard Roman procedure (Sherwin-White [1963] p. 48). The charges brought against Paul were, he says, just disagreements **about their peculiar religion** (v. 19), surprising and strong language for the author of *Acts* to put in Festus' mouth when addressing Agrippa, who (whatever his private attitudes may have been) was officially a devout Jew. Haenchen and Bruce therefore render this Greek word, *deisidaimonia* (= fear of supernatural beings), by the neutral 'religion', but the word commonly carries the same pejorative overtones as the Latin *superstitio*; on the other hand, when Paul is speaking at the Areopagus in Athens (17.22), he describes the Athenians using a related word *deisidaimonesterous*, in circumstances where presumably he is not being represented as insulting or provocative. Paul then, he said, declined an invitation to stand trial in Jerusalem, and instead appealed for the matter to be referred to the emperor's **decision** (v. 21), using the Greek word *diagnosis* as the equivalent of the Latin legal term *cognitio* (= jurisdiction); see Sherwin-White (1963) pp. 17ff.

Agrippa agrees to help Festus by hearing the prisoner, and next day Paul is brought in escorted by **high-ranking officers and prominent citizens** (v. 23). The 'high-ranking officers' are in fact *chiliarchoi* (see note on 21.31). BC (IV, p. 312) and Bruce (p. 493) refer to Josephus' statement (*Ant.* 19, 365-6) that five cohorts of infantry, recruited locally, remained in Judaea after 44. But these can hardly all have been cohorts of Roman citizens or 1,000 strong (see note on 21.31), so that their commanders would have been called *praefecti*. The author of *Acts* is using *chiliar-*

chos to cover all commanders of auxiliary cohorts, regardless of their actual title. Presumably the mention of 'prominent citizens' is another instance of the author's desire to represent Paul as being on good terms with the highest classes in society.

Although Sherwin-White (1963, p. 64) denies that Festus' words, **I decided to send him** (v. 25) to Caesar, necessarily imply that Festus had the discretion to send or not to send Paul to the emperor, it is difficult not to conclude from the combination of this statement with v. 12 above that the author of *Acts* assumed that Festus did have that discretion (see note on 25.12).

Festus needs Agrippa's help in composing some sort of account of the charges to be sent to Rome with Paul. He wishes Agrippa to hear him **so that as a result of this preliminary enquiry I may have something to report** (v. 26). This enquiry (*anakrisis* is the word used) is thus not a further judicial hearing but a search for information. The 3rd century jurist Marcian wrote that 'after an appeal has been made, letters should be sent by the person from whom appeal is made to the person who will hear the appeal, whether he be the emperor or someone else' (*Digest* 49, 6, 1, pr.).

Chapter 26

Paul gives an account of his conversion; Agrippa decides that he is harmless.

Paul's speech essentially repeats the same points he has made earlier, but at greater length and in much more stylish Greek. Though directed at a Jew (Agrippa) and addressing Jewish issues (e.g. vv. 4-8), there is a notable lack of Biblical references and Septuagint language, until the speech of Jesus in Paul's vision in vv. 15-18. We are given the third account of his conversion, the second from his own mouth (9.3-9; 22.6-11). It omits the rôle of Ananias, but is the only account to include the famous words of Jesus, **It is hard for you, this kicking against the goad** (v. 14; a phrase which has parallels in Greek and Latin literature, but not in the Bible nor, so far as one can tell, in any other contemporary Jewish writings: cf. Aeschylus, *Agamemnon* 1624; *Prometheus Vinctus* 323; Pindar, *Pythia* 2, 94-6; Euripides, *Bacchae* 795; Terence, *Phormio* 78). It is a speech appropriate to a very Hellenised king.

In response to Festus' exasperated outburst, **you are raving** (v. 24), Paul's reply contains a carefully-worded compliment to Agrippa: **the king is well versed in these matters, and to him I can speak freely** (v. 26). The Greek has two verbs in the last section of this sentence, 'I speak, using freedom of speech (*parrhesiazomenos*)'. The noun *parrhesia*, and the verb derived from it, become almost technical terms in politics under the rule of the emperors; a 'good' emperor would tolerate *parrhesia* from his subjects, while a subject who used *parrhesia* regardless of the emperor's (or the governor's) attitude was to be admired (see J. Crook, *Consilium Principis*, pp. 142-7); so Paul's compliment to Agrippa is also the author's compliment to Paul.

Paul's audience come to the conclusion that Paul is harmless. **Agrippa said to Festus, 'The fellow could have been discharged, if he had not appealed to the emperor'** (v. 32). Whereas 25.12 and 25 imply that Festus had discretion to send Paul to Rome for trial or to try him himself (see note on 25.25), this implies that, once he had agreed to transfer the case, he no longer had the right to rule that Paul had no case to answer (cf. note on 25.12).

Chapter 27

Paul and his escort embark for Italy; they are shipwrecked on Malta.

For the journey to Italy, Paul is put in the charge of **a centurion named Julius, of the Augustan cohort** (v. 1). Auxiliary cohorts often carried an honorific epithet, and 'Augustan' was one such epithet. A *cohors* I *Augusta Lusitanorum* was stationed in Judaea in AD 86 (Schürer[2] I, p. 367, n. 67). The suggestion (Schürer[2] I, p. 364) that one of the five infantry cohorts of Sebasteni organised by Agrippa (see note on 23.23) had the honorific title *Augusta* is entirely speculative. The 'we' reappears in this verse.

They take passage in **a ship of Adramyttium** (v. 2; Adramyttium is on the western coast of Asia Minor, east of Assos) which was no doubt trading up and down the coast (cf. 20.13-16), and after a brief stop in Sidon, arrive at Myra in Lycia, where **the centurion found an Alexandrian vessel bound for Italy, and put us aboard** (v. 6). The ship is presumably bound for Puteoli (see note on 28.13); we learn later that it was carrying corn (v. 38) and that it was very large (v. 37). Since the annexation of Egypt by Rome in 30 BC, corn had been exported in large quantities from Egypt to help feed the huge population of Rome; under Augustus some 133,000 tonnes of wheat were exported (perhaps more than half the total Egyptian production; see P. Garnsey, *Famine and Food Supply in the Greco-Roman World*, p. 231). A substantial fleet was responsible for conveying this grain to Rome; the ships were owned by private entrepreneurs, not by the Roman state. Claudius is known to have offered privileges to ship-owners who would undertake to transport grain to Rome for six years.

Note that the centurion, although on official business, travels with his prisoner on an ordinary merchant vessel, exactly as Paul had done on his earlier journeys; but then Paul must have had to bargain with the owners or masters for his passage. The centurion, on the other hand, could compel them to give himself, his prisoners, and his escort of soldiers (vv. 31-2, 42) passage. Officials, soldiers, and couriers travelling on official business had, from the time of Augustus onwards, been supplied with passes called *diplomata* which empowered them to require the civilian population to help them on their way. There is plentiful evidence of what happened on land; individuals could be taken from their work to act as guides (hence Jesus' remark 'if a man in authority makes you go one mile, go with him two': Matt. 5.41), cities billetted the visitors in private homes, and animals and waggons were requisitioned to transport them and their baggage (and so were river boats on the Nile: Hunt and Edgar, *Select Papyri* II, no. 211, ll. 10-21). See Williams, *Pliny's Correspondence with Trajan*, pp. 105-6. The centurion presumably could not order a local merchant ship to take them all the way to Rome, but he could commandeer places on a ship which was going there anyway, and would hardly venture to interfere with the course it took, until an emergency arose (see v. 11). Even governors or emperors might use commercial ships. There is a letter of Hadrian of 129 asking the archons and *Boule* of Ephesus to admit to the Council Lucius Erastus: 'he says that he frequently sails the sea...and always conveys the governors of the province (i.e. Asia); and he has now twice voyaged with myself, first when I was carried from Rhodes to Ephesus, and now when I have come to you from Eleusis' (*Sylloge* 838, ll. 6-11).

The voyage from Puteoli to Alexandria followed the prevailing winds, and was very quick; Pliny the Elder (*Natural History* 19, 3), records an exceptional crossing taking only nine days, but two or three weeks would have been more usual. Philo (*In Flaccum* 26) reports that the emperor Gaius advised Herod Agrippa I (see note on 12.1) to travel back to Syria by taking a ship from Puteoli to Alexandria, because there were on that route 'very fast merchant-ships, with skilled captains who drive them as a charioteer drives his team, and provide a straight passage on the direct route'. Returning, however, the winds were against them. Ancient ships could tack, but not very efficiently. Normally, then, they would take a route either to the south, by way of Cyrene and North Africa, or to the north by way of Cyprus, Myra, Rhodes or Cnidos, Malta, and Messina (which is why the centurion thought that Myra was a good place to pick up a ship to Puteoli). That journey could take one or two months.

The Egyptian harvest would be over by May, but there would normally not be time to thresh it and dry it and load it on the ships in time to get it to Rome before the sailing season ended in November. They would therefore sail from Alexandria in April, arriving in Puteoli in May or June. Then, if they were lucky, they could unload quickly and return to Alexandria in time to load another cargo and make another run before the season ended.

It would be for the captain to judge whether there was time, and the weather would hold long enough, to make that second run; the alternative was to spend the winter in port at Alexandria. In the case of the ship which Paul took (and the one which took him on from Malta: 28.11) the captain miscalculated (L. Casson, *Ships and Seamanship in the Ancient World*, pp. 297-9).

The first part of the journey, to **Cnidus** (v. 7), on a peninsula on the south-western tip of Asia Minor, goes badly because the wind is against them, so they sail south-west, round **Salmone** (v. 7) on the eastern end of Crete, in the hope that the island of Crete will provide some shelter from the wind. When they have got as far as **a place called Fair Havens, not far from the town of Lasea** (v. 8), which is probably just west of Lebena in the centre of the southern coast of Crete, it is apparent that time is running out; **the Fast was already over** (v. 9), which meant (if the reference is to the Fast of the Day of Atonement) that they were well into the period when navigation was becoming dangerous, and approaching November, when all sailing ceased (Bruce, p. 515). Paul (v. 10) warns against going on, but the **centurion paid more attention to the captain and to the owner of the ship** (v. 11). Although the centurion was in principle just a passenger, his status as the holder of an official *diploma* (see note on v. 6) would give him the final say in this emergency. In any case, he had soldiers under his command who would enforce his wishes (vv. 31-2), even against their own inclinations (vv. 42-3). On land, civilians who resisted soldiers carrying out requisitions could be handled very roughly; Epictetus said that, when a soldier commandeered a donkey, its owner should not resist, or even grumble, or he would be beaten up and still lose his donkey (*Diss.* 4, 1, 79).

The captain (Greek *kybernetes*) would be the professional sailor in charge of the management of the ship and the crew, and the owner (Greek *naukleros*) is the person who has the use of the ship, either because it is his, or because he has chartered it (L. Casson, *Ships and Seamanship in the Ancient World*, pp. 314-18). It is not said what Paul wants them to do instead of trying to sail further west along the coast **to winter at Phoenix** (v. 12), if indeed the harbour at Fair Havens was **unsuitable for wintering** (v. 12). By now they seem to have given up hope of completing the voyage that season; did Paul wish them to abandon ship?

When a southerly wind springs up they set sail for Phoenix, but are caught by **a fierce wind, the 'North-easter' as they call it** (v. 14); in Greek, the name of the wind is *Eurakulon*, a word which is attested nowhere else, and which seems to be a compound of the Greek *Euros* (= the east wind) and the Latin *Aquilo* (= the north wind). The Latin form *Euroaquilo* appears on a pavement adjacent to the forum in Dougga (in modern Tunisia) which represents the directions of the winds (Bruce, p. 518); its position there suggests a north-northeast wind, but (as Bruce, loc. cit., suggests) something more like a east-northeasterly wind is required to drive the ship past the island of **Cauda** (v. 16; some manuscripts have *Clauda* instead, and both forms of the name are attested in ancient authorities), and then threaten to carry them **to the shallows of Syrtis** (v. 17), notoriously dangerous waters off the Libyan coast in the gulf between Cyrene and Carthage.

The ship is now made ready to weather the storm. First they **managed to get the ship's boat under control** (v. 16) by hoisting it on board, a natural precaution. The significance of the next process, **they made use of tackle and undergirded the ship** (v. 17), cannot be determined with any certainty. 'Tackle' translates the Greek *boetheia* (= help, aid); some kind of aid in managing the ship is meant, but the word is of no help in clarifying the process. 'Undergirded' represents the Greek *hypozonnuntes*; a piece of equipment known as a *hypozoma* was carried by triremes in the 5th century BC; it is now generally accepted that this was a double rope within the hull of the ship (but low down, hence the 'under' part of the word), running from the stern to the stem, which was tightened to brace the ship's timbers (see J.S. Morrison and J.F. Coates, *The Athenian Trireme*, pp. 170-2); running a rope *within* the ship, however, does not seem practical for a vessel loaded with cargo, and it may be that the word refers to 'frapping', passing cables under the ship to strengthen a weakened hull (L. Casson, *Ships and Seamanship in the Ancient World*, pp. 91-2).

They **lowered the mainsail** (v. 17), or perhaps 'dropped a sea-anchor' (Haenchen p. 703, n. 2; the Greek simply says 'let go the gear'). After lightening ship (vv. 18-19) they attempt to ride out the storm. When **the fourteenth night came** (v. 27) soundings reveal that land may be near, so, in order to avoid shipwreck, they attempt to check its movement by dropping **four anchors from the stern** (v. 29). Ancient ships carried large numbers of anchors, which varied from simple stones to devices very like modern anchors (see L. Casson, *Ships and Seamanship in the Ancient World*, pp. 252-6). The sailors next attempt to **lay out anchors from the bows** (v. 30), and take to the ship's boat, no doubt intending to drop the anchors away from the ship so that the cables can be hauled in to let the anchors get purchase on the sea-bed, and steady the ship. Paul, however, believes (for reasons which are not explained) that they are trying to abandon ship (an extremely foolish thing to do in a small boat, at night, during a storm, off an unknown coast), and persuades his escort to intervene by cutting the boat's ropes and casting it adrift.

We are told that the number of people on the boat was **two hundred and seventy six** (v. 37). Although some manuscripts have seventy six instead, there is no need to doubt the larger number. Some of the Alexandrian grain ships were very large indeed; Lucian (*Navigium* 5) describes one 180 feet long, with a beam of 45 feet, and 44 feet deep, carrying perhaps 1,300 tons of grain (L. Casson, *The Ancient Mariners*, pp. 208-9); the ship in which Josephus was wrecked on the way to Rome in 64 (*Life* 15) had about six hundred people on board. They **lightened the ship by dumping the corn in the sea** (v. 38). This would be a difficult process if it involved emptying the hold; if, however, corn was stored in sacks on the deck, jettisoning it would improve both the buoyancy and the stability of the ship. Finally, seeing a good beach nearby they drive the ship ashore.

Chapter 28

The travellers are treated kindly by the natives; Paul survives a snake-bite; he heals the father of the chief magistrate; they arrive at Rome; he addresses the Roman Jews; he remains in Rome openly teaching for two years.

Having reached the shore they **identified the island as Malta** (v. 1); in Greek the name is *Melite* (or in some manuscripts *Melitene* or *Melitine*). It had passed from Carthaginian to Roman suzerainty in 218 BC and came under the authority of the proconsuls of Sicily. The **rough islanders** (v. 2) who receive them with kindness are in Greek *barbaroi*, a term conventionally translated 'barbarians' though actually meaning no more than that they spoke neither Latin nor Greek. There is evidence that Punic had been the language on the island (BC IV, p. 340); modern Maltese is a Semitic language probably closely related to Arabic.

There are two inscriptions from Malta, one in Greek and one in Latin, which suggest that in using the term **the chief magistrate of the island** (v. 7) the author may be reproducing an official title (BC IV, p. 342); but there is no further evidence about the powers or duties of such an official. He has a Roman personal name, Publius.

Their three months stay on Malta would bring them to February (see 27.9) when, according to Pliny the Elder (*Natural History* 2, 122) the sailing season begins again. They take passage in **a ship which had wintered in the island; she was the *Castor and Pollux* of Alexandria** (v. 11). For the Alexandrian grain fleet, see note on 27.6. Presumably this ship has been unable to complete the journey back to Puteoli in the face of unfavourable winds, and has been forced to lay up in Malta. She is taking the earliest opportunity to complete her voyage. The Greek actually says that her *parasemon* was the *Dioskouroi*, that is to say, the two sons of Zeus, Castor and Pollux. Just as today, ships in antiquity bore names, and are referred to by those names in legal documents and religious dedications. Almost all of the names of merchant ships which we know are of gods.

The Dioscuri gave their name to more than one vessel, probably because they were regarded as the protectors of seamen (the earliest reference to this function of the Dioscuri is in [Homer] *Hymns* 33, ll. 6-17, but it is commonly referred to in later literature, e.g. Horace, *Odes* 1, 12, ll. 25-32; the phenomenon of 'St Elmo's fire', a bluish light which sometimes appears on ships' masts, was regarded as a sign of their protection: Pliny the Elder, *Natural History* 2, 101). A *parasemon* was a normal feature of ships, a device carved usually at the prow representing her name and identifying her. Lucian (*Navigium* 5) describes the ship *Isis* as having 'a prow with Isis, after whom the ship was named, on both sides'.

She sails first to **Syracuse** (v. 12), on the east coast of Sicily, and the most important city in the province, from there to **Rhegium** (v. 13), the city at the southernmost tip of Italy, just across the Straits of Messina from Sicily (modern Reggio di Calabria), and finally they catch a favourable wind and in two days arrive at their destination, **Puteoli** (v. 13), modern Pozzuoli on the northern coast of the Bay of Naples. Before the development of adequate harbour facilities at Ostia at the mouth of the Tiber under Claudius large vessels with cargoes for Rome regularly landed them at Puteoli; it was the normal port for the Alexandrian grain ships. Seneca (*Ep. Mor.* 77, 1; for Seneca see note on 18.12) describes the arrival at Puteoli of the season's first ships from Alexandria: 'the whole of Puteoli crowded onto the wharves, all picking out the Alexandrian vessels from an immense crowd of other shipping by the trim of their sails'. In the last years of his life, the emperor Augustus was gratified when, on the way to Capri, the passengers and crew of an Alexandrian ship burnt incense in his honour and praised his beneficence; he showed his gratitude by giving his staff a substantial tip, which they had to promise they would spend only on Alexandrian goods (Suetonius, *Augustus* 98). It was not only corn which was carried; Nero made himself very unpopular when, during a food shortage, an Alexandrian ship put in and unloaded, not corn, but sand for the emperor's wrestlers (Suetonius, *Nero* 45). Puteoli was a prosperous and cosmopolitan sea port; it is the setting for the well-known Banquet of Trimalchio in Petronius' satirical novel, *Satyricon* (26-78). It is therefore not surprising that Paul should find **fellow-Christians** (ch. 14) there; they, or the message of Christianity, would travel quickly to a place with trade connections all over the Mediterranean.

Paul and his escort will have completed the journey to Rome overland, along the Appian way, on which **Appii Forum and Tres Tabernae** (v. 15) lie. There he is met by the Roman Christians, who will know of Paul from his letter to them. The origins of the Roman community are not stated, but the long list of names mentioned by Paul in ch. 16 of *Romans* suggests both that it was large and that it had good connections with Christians elsewhere.

In Rome, **Paul was allowed to lodge by himself with a soldier in charge of him** (v. 16). In a letter to Antioch the emperor Antoninus Pius wrote that 'the man who is prepared to furnish guarantors should not be put into chains unless it is accepted that he committed a crime so serious that he should not be entrusted either to guarantors or to soldiers' (*Digest* 48, 3, 3). The jurist Ulpian said that 'in the matter of the custody of accused persons a proconsul is accustomed to assess whether an individual should be put into prison or be entrusted to a soldier, or to guarantors, or to himself' (*Digest* 48, 3, 1). These and other passages (*Digest* 2, 11, 4, 1; 4, 6, 10) show that Roman law had a third method of dealing with accused persons in addition to those used in modern Britain, remand in custody ('chains' or 'prison' in the texts above) and release on bail ('guarantors' in the texts above), namely being guarded outside prison by a soldier. This was clearly the method used in Paul's case at Rome.

Paul is represented as being on good terms with the local Jews, and remains in Rome **two full years** (v. 30) teaching **openly and without hindrance** (v. 31). We are not told what happened at the end of the two years. For a discussion of the ending of *Acts*, see Introduction pp. 6-7.

Eusebius (*Ecclesiastical History* 2, 22) says that 'Paul's martyrdom was not accomplished during the stay at Rome described by Luke'. In fact there was a tradition that Paul lived on to undertake more missionary journeys; the Pastoral Epistles (which, even if they are not by Paul, are evidence of early tradition) refer to journeys to Nicopolis (Tit. 3.12) and further visits to the cities of the east (1 Tim. 1.3; 2 Tim. 4.13, 20); *Romans* (15.28) speaks of an intention to go to Spain. According to Eusebius (*Ecclesiastical History* 2, 25) under Nero 'Paul was beheaded in Rome itself' (traditionally at Tre Fontane on the Via Ostiensis); he quotes authorities for this view from the 2nd century. His supposed burial place was marked by a small shrine, which was replaced in the late 4th century by the great church of San Paolo fuori le mura.

Appendix

Scenes from *Acts* depicted by Western painters

The narrative of *Acts* inspired far fewer pictures than the central events of the Gospels (as one would expect), and it was also less popular than parts of the Old Testament and the lives of such saints as Francis of Assisi. Nevertheless it provided subjects for some of the works which marked turning-points in Italian Renaissance painting: Masaccio's frescoes in the Brancacci Chapel in S. Maria del Carmine at Florence; the youthful Mantegna's first great cycle in the Ovetari Chapel in the Eremitani Church at Padua (destroyed by bombing in 1944); Raphael's cartoons for tapestries for the Sistine Chapel; one of Michelangelo's two last paintings in the Vatican.

REF.	SUBJECT	PAINTER	LOCATION
2.1-4	Pentecost	Titian	Venice, S. Maria della Salute
2.38	St Peter preaching repentance and baptism	Masolino (perhaps with Masaccio)	Florence, Brancacci Chapel
2.41	St Peter baptising converts	Masaccio (perhaps with Masolino)	Florence, Brancacci Chapel
3.1-10	St Peter healing a lame man	Masolino	Florence, Brancacci Chapel
		Raphael	London, Victoria & Albert Museum
		Poussin	New York, Metropolitan Museum

4.32-5.6	The distribution of alms and the death of Ananias	Masaccio	Florence, Brancacci Chapel
5.7-10	The death of Sapphira	Poussin	Paris, Louvre
5.15	The healing of the sick by Peter's shadow	Masaccio	Florence, Brancacci Chapel
7.54-60	The stoning of Stephen	Tapestry after Raphael	Vatican, Pinacoteca
		Elsheimer	Edinburgh, National Gallery
8.27-39	The baptism of the Ethiopian eunuch by Philip	Claude	Cardiff, National Museum
9.1-7	The conversion of Saul	Tapestry after Raphael	Vatican, Pinacoteca
		Michelangelo	Vatican, Capella Paolina
		Caravaggio	Rome, S. Maria del,, Popolo
9.36-43	The raising of Tabitha by Peter	Masolino	Florence, Brancacci Chapel
12.2	Trial and execution of James	Mantegna	Padua, Ovetari Chapel (destroyed in 1944)
12.6-11	Peter delivered from prison	Raphael	Vatican, Stanza d'Eliodoro
		Filippino Lippi	Florence, Brancacci Chapel
13.6-12	The blinding of Elymas	Raphael	London, Victoria & Albert Museum
14.7-18	The sacrifice at Lystra	Raphael	London, Victoria & Albert Museum
16.25-6	The earthquake at Philippi	Tapestry after Raphael	Vatican, Pinacoteca

17.16-34	Paul preaching at Athens	Raphael	London, Victoria & Albert Museum
27.1-2	Paul's embarkation at Caesarea	Claude	Birmingham, City Museum & Gallery
28.2-6	Paul bitten by a snake at Malta	Benjamin West	Greenwich, Royal Naval College Chapel
		Elsheimer	Frankfurt, Stadelsches Institut

Bibliography

Abbreviations used for commentaries, works frequently cited,
and reference works.

BC = Foakes Jackson, F.J. and Lake, K., *The Beginnings of Christianity,
Part 1: The Acts of the Apostles* (Macmillan, 5 vols, 1920-33; repr.
Baker Book House, 1979).

Bruce = Bruce, F.F., *The Acts of the Apostles: the Greek Text with Commentary* (3rd edn, Apollos, 1990).

Dessau = Dessau, H., *Inscriptiones Latinae Selectae* (Weidmann, 1892-
1916).

Haenchen = Haenchen, E., *The Acts of the Apostles* (Blackwell, 1971).

OGIS = Dittenberger, W., *Orientis Graeci Inscriptiones Selectae* (Georg
Olms, 1960).

Schürer[2] = Schürer, E., *The History of the Jewish People in the Age of
Jesus Christ* (3 vols), revised and edited by G. Vermes and F. Millar (T.
& T. Clark Ltd, 1973-87).

Sherwin-White (1963) = Sherwin-White, A.N., *Roman Society and Roman
Law in the New Testament* (Clarendon Press, 1963).

Sylloge = Dittenberger, W., *Sylloge Inscriptionum Graecarum* (Georg
Olms, 1960).

General bibliography

Applebaum, S., *Jews and Greeks in Ancient Cyrene* (Brill, 1979).

Barnes, T.D., 'Legislation against the Christians' *Journal of Roman
Studies* 58 (1968) pp. 32-50.

———— 'An Apostle on Trial' *Journal of Theological Studies* 20 (1969)
pp. 407-19.

Bowers, W.P., 'Paul's Route through Mysia: A Note on *Acts* XVI' *Journal
of Theological Studies* 30 (1979) pp. 507-11.

Bowersock, G.W., *Greek Sophists in the Roman Empire* (Clarendon Press,
1969).

Bowker, J., *Jesus and the Pharisees* (Cambridge University Press, 1973).

Braudel, F., *The Mediterranean and the Mediterranean World in the Age of Philip II* (Collins, 1972-3).

Bruce, F.F., 'Christianity under Claudius' *Bulletin of the John Rylands Library* 44 (1961-2) pp. 309-26.

———— 'Galatian Problems 2' *Bulletin of the John Rylands Library* 52 (1969-70) pp. 243-66.

———— 'Galatian Problems 4' *Bulletin of the John Rylands Library* 54 (1971-2) pp. 250-67.

———— *Paul, Apostle of the Free Spirit* (The Paternoster Press, 1977).

Burton, G.P., 'Proconsuls, Assizes and the Administration of Justice under the Empire' *Journal of Roman Studies* 65 (1975) pp. 92-106.

Cadbury, H.J., *Style and Literary Method of Luke* (*Harvard Theological Studies* 6, 1919 and 1920).

Calder, W.M., *Monumenta Asiae Minoris Antiqua* vol. 7 (Manchester University Press, 1956).

Camp, J.M., *The Athenian Agora: Excavations in the Heart of Classical Athens* (Thames and Hudson, 1986).

Casson, L., *Ships and Seamanship in the Ancient World* (Princeton University Press, 1971).

———— *The Ancient Mariners* (Princeton University Press, 1991).

Crook, J.A., *Consilium Principis* (Cambridge University Press, 1955).

———— *Law and Life of Rome* (Thames and Hudson, 1967).

Cullman, O., *The Christology of the New Testament* (SCM Press, 1959).

Davies, W.D., and Finkelstein, L., *The Cambridge History of Judaism* (Cambridge University Press, 1984-9).

Deissman, A., *Light from the Ancient East* (Hodder and Stoughton, 1927).

De Ste. Croix, G.E.M., *The Class Struggle in the Ancient Greek World* (Duckworth, 1981).

———— 'Early Christian Attitudes to Property and Slavery' in D. Baker (ed.), *Studies in Church History* vol. 12 (Blackwell, 1975) pp. 1-38.

Dibelius, M., *Studies in the Acts of the Apostles* (SCM Press, 1956).

Fage, J.D. (ed.), *The Cambridge History of Africa* vol. II: ca. 500 BC-AD 1050 (Cambridge University Press, 1978).

Finley, M.I., *The World of Odysseus* (Chatto and Windus, 2nd edn, 1967).

———— 'The Trojan War' *Journal of Hellenic Studies* 84 (1964) pp. 1-9.

———— *The Ancient Economy* (Chatto and Windus, 1973).

Finnegan, J., *Handbook of Biblical Chronology* (Princeton University Press, 1964).

Garnsey, P., 'The Criminal Jurisdiction of Governors' *Journal of Roman Studies* 58 (1968) pp. 51-9.

———— *Social Status and Legal Privilege in the Roman Empire* (Clarendon Press, 1970).

———— *Famine and Food Supply in the Graeco-Roman World* (Cambridge University Press, 1988).

Geagan, D.W., *The Athenian Constitution after Sulla* (*Hesperia* Supplement 12, 1967).

———— 'Roman Athens: Some Aspects of Life and Culture' in H. Temporini (ed.), *Aufstieg und Niedergang der Römischen Welt* II 7.1 (Walter de Gruyter, 1979) pp. 371-437.

Goodman, M., *The Ruling Class of Judaea* (Cambridge University Press, 1987).

Graindor, P., *Athènes d'Auguste à Trajan* (Le Caire, 1934).

Habicht, C., 'New evidence on the Province of Asia' *Journal of Roman Studies* 65 (1975) pp. 64-91.

Harnack, A., *Luke the Physician* (Williams and Norgate, 1907).

Head, B.V., *Historia Nummorum* (Clarendon Press, 2nd edn, 1911).

Hemer, C.J., 'Paul at Athens' *New Testament Studies* 20 (1974) pp. 341-50.

———— 'The Adjective "Phrygia" ' *Journal of Theological Studies* 27 (1976) pp. 122-6.

———— 'Phrygia: a further note' *Journal of Theological Studies* 28 (1977) pp. 99-101.

———— 'Alexandria Troas' *Tyndale Bulletin* 26 (1975) pp. 79-112.

Hicks, E.L., *Ancient Greek Inscriptions in the British Museum* (Clarendon Press, 1874-1916).

Holder, P.A., *The Auxilia from Augustus to Trajan* (British Archaeological Reports, International Series 70, 1980).

Hollis, A.S., *Ovid: Metamorphoses VIII* (Clarendon Press, 1970).

Hopkins, K., 'Taxes and Trade in the Roman Empire (200 BC-AD 400)' *Journal of Roman Studies* 70 (1980) pp. 101-25.

Hunt, A.S. and Edgar, C.C., *Select Papyri* (Heinemann, 1932-4).

Jameson, S., 'The Lycian League: Some Problems in its Administration' in H. Temporini (ed.), *Aufstieg und Niedergang der Römischen Welt* II 7.2 (Walter de Gruyter, 1980) pp. 832-55.

Jones, A.H.M., *The Greek City from Alexander to Justinian* (Clarendon Press, 1940).

———— *Studies in Roman Government and Law* (Blackwell, 1960).

———— *The Criminal Courts of the Roman Republic and Principate* (Blackwell, 1973).

———— *Cities of the Eastern Roman Provinces* (Clarendon Press, 1937; 2nd edn, 1971).

Larsen, J.A.O., *Representative Government in Greek and Roman History* (California University Press, 1966).

Levick, B., *Roman Colonies in Southern Asia Minor* (Clarendon Press, 1967).

Lewis, D.M., Review of J.N. Sevenster, *Do You Know Greek?*, *Journal of Theological Studies* 20 (1969) pp. 584-8.

Lewis, N., and Reinhold, M., *Roman Civilisation, a Sourcebook* (Harper Torchbooks, 1966).

MacMullen, R., *Roman Social Relations* (Yale University Press, 1974).

―――― *Christianizing the Roman Empire* (Yale University Press, 1984).

Marrou, H.I., *A History of Education in Antiquity* (Sheed and Ward, 1956).

Mason, H.J., *Greek Terms for Roman Institutions* (Hakkert, 1974).

Meeks, W.A., *The First Urban Christians* (Yale University Press, 1983).

Merkelbach, R., 'Ephesische Parerga (18); der Bäckerstreik' *Zeitschrift für Papyrologie und Epigraphik* 30 (1970) pp. 164-5.

Millar, F., *The Emperor in the Roman World* (Duckworth, 1977).

Mitchell, S., 'Iconium and Ninica' *Historia* 28 (1979) pp. 409-38.

Morrison, J.S., and Coates, J.F., *The Athenian Trireme* (Cambridge University Press, 1986).

Musurillo, H., *Acts of the Christian Martyrs* (Clarendon Press, 1972).

Nock, A.D., *Essays on Religion in the Ancient World* (Clarendon Press, 1972).

Oliver, J.H., 'The Epistle of Claudius which Mentions the Proconsul Junius Gallio' *Hesperia* 40 (1971) pp. 239-40.

Plassart, A., *Fouilles de Delphes* III iv (1970) no. 286.

―――― 'L'Inscription de Delphes Mentionnant le Proconsul Gallio' *Revue des Etudes Grecques* 80 (1967) pp. 372-8.

Price, M.J., and Trell, B.L., *Coins and their Cities* (Vecchi, 1977).

Rajak, T., *Josephus* (Duckworth, 1983).

―――― 'Was there a Roman Charter for Jews?' *Journal of Roman Studies* 74 (1984) pp. 107-23.

Ramsay, W.M., *The Church in the Roman Empire* (5th edn, Hodder and Stoughton, 1897).

―――― *St. Paul the Traveller and the Roman Citizen* (Hodder and Stoughton, 1895).

Reynolds, J., 'Hadrian, Antoninus Pius, and the Cyrenaican Cities' *Journal of Roman Studies* 68 (1978) pp. 111-21.

―――― *Aphrodisias and Rome* (Society for the Promotion of Roman Studies, 1982).

Reynolds, J., and Tannenbaum, R., 'Jews and Godfearers at Aphrodisias' *Proceedings of the Cambridge Philological Society* suppl. vol. 12 (1987).

Robert, L., 'Sur des inscriptions d' Ephèse. Fêtes, athlètes, empereurs, épigrammes' *Revue de Philologie* 41 (1967) pp. 7-84.

Robinson, J.A.T., *Redating the New Testament* (SCM Press Ltd, 1976).

Rostovtzeff, M., *Social and Economic History of the Roman Empire* (2nd edn, Clarendon Press, 1957).

Safrai, S., and Stern, M. (eds), *The Jewish People in the 1st Century* (Van Gorcum, 1974-6).

Sevenster, J.N., *Do You Know Greek?* (Brill, 1968; suppl. to *Novum Testamentum* vol. XIX).

Sherk, R.K., *Roman Documents from the Greek East* (Johns Hopkins University Press, 1969).

———— *Rome and the Greek East* (Cambridge University Press, 1984).

Sherwin-White, A.N., *The Letters of Pliny: A Historical and Social Commentary* (Clarendon Press, 1966).

———— *Racial Prejudice in Imperial Rome* (Cambridge University Press, 1967).

Smallwood, E.M., *Documents Illustrating the Principates of Nerva, Trajan and Hadrian* (Cambridge University Press, 1966).

———— *The Jews under Roman Rule* (Brill, 1976)

Stillwell, R. (ed.), *Princeton Encyclopedia of Classical Sites* (Princeton University Press, 1976).

Watson, G.R., *The Roman Soldier* (Thames and Hudson, 1969).

Williams, W., *Pliny the Younger: Correspondence with Trajan from Bithynia (Epistles X)* (Aris and Phillips, 1990).

Wilson, S.G., *Luke and the Law* (Cambridge University Press, 1983).

Wycherley, R.E., 'St. Paul at Athens' *Journal of Theological Studies* 19 (1968) pp. 619-21.

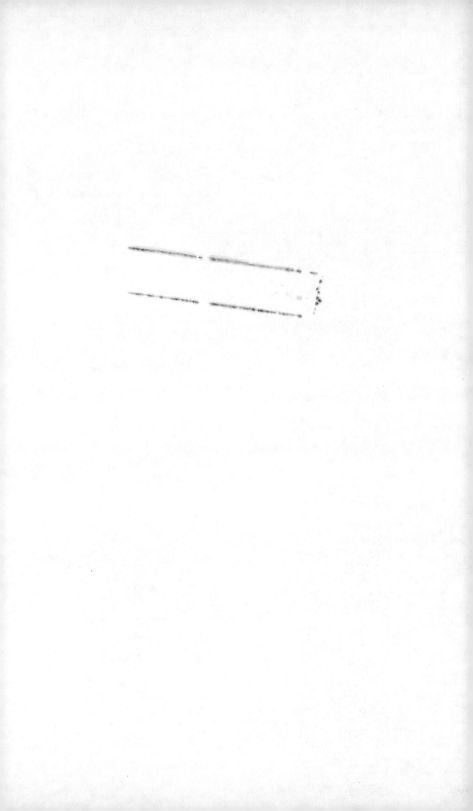